Under 2 flags

Under 2 flags

Pictures of a Life
between
Heidelberg and Hollywood

George P. Richardson, Ph.D.

To order additional copies of this book, contact:
Xlibris LLC
0-800-056-3182
www.xlibrispublishing.co.uk
Orders@xlibrispublishing.co.uk
307203

Contents

To Hildburg

Prologue

I have often been approached by friends and acquaintances to write about my unusual and exciting life in order to share these experiences.

I have almost worked a year on this biography which I shared with Richard W. Cordano E.D.D., who was former Director and Principal of Arcadia High School, where I was active as Vice Director during my career in education.

He forwarded the following lines, which I believe that no one else could have phrased more appropriately.

December 11.2012

Hello George:

I just finished reading your book and it was great from beginning to end.

Congratulations on putting together a written memory of your very exciting life. I had no idea of your background and the two different cultures. It's funny, but you work with a person for all those years and never really get to know anything about him. For instance, I did not know you were in the army and was a veteran, I knew that Col. Melon was in the air force and that Rex Welty was a major in the army, Lloyd Savage a Lt. Comdr. in the Navy, Cub Conover in the Coast Guard, but that's about the extent of my knowledge.

Your experiences with horses were also news to me; being a city boy myself, I have only ridden a horse twice in my life. Your riding for movie stars is mind blowing, wow—you should have been bragging about it everyday.

Thank you for the kind words and references to Arcadia High School. As you know, I loved the place dearly and always appreciate hearing that others felt the same way, sorry to say, a few on the AHS staff didn't feel the same way. But as an Administrator you know you cannot please them all.

I reviewed the contents of the book with Elb and Fred Nahra with whom I have coffee with every Friday, and they too enjoyed what you wrote about them and the school.

What are your plans now as an author, are you going to publish this book and write some more because you are good at it, or are off to other pursuits? Keep in touch and if you are in Pasadena over the holidays, give me a call and join us for coffee.

We would enjoy seeing you.

All The Best

When one recalls events after such a long time and tries to put in on paper, then it's possible that there are gaps in the events and there are also names that I have forgotten. Many items like photos and documents were destroyed as the result of the events of war.

I surely could not have completed this book without the support of these nominated persons:

Irene Atkinson, was very helpful as secretary of the English text

Florian Moeller, who initially translated the English text into German and finally,

Magdalena Bergen–Gerdes and **Horst Gerdes,** who traveled from Germany to help me complete the final version of my biography in German and English

The way it all started

My father was the youngest son of an Orthodox priest from Strumica, Macedonia. My grandfather, as was customary in those days, preached from the pulpit and carried a rifle to go after the Turks. In the Balkans, the Turks were masters and the rest of the Christians were go-alongs. In the pursuit of his patriotic duties as a Macedonian, he was killed. My Uncle Chris, the older brother of my father, was able to escape the Turks by going through the Austrian-Hungarian Empire, the Trieste, and then to the United States. There he eventually established a bakery factory in Detroit. Detroit at the time was a very significant location for Macedonians and Bulgarians. My father was, as the saying goes, "rescued by the Greek Orthodox" and put into a monastery where he was taught classic Greek and Latin. He spoke Macedonian and he knew how to write Macedonian, so he was not illiterate in that sense. Eventually, following the lead of Uncle Chris, he was also able to migrate through the Austrian-Hungarian Empire, i.e. Trieste, to the United States.

My mother was German by birth. Yes, she was an Austrian-Hungarian. My mother's father attended the Royal Imperial Cadet Schools in Vienna, Prague, and Budapest. However, his perfect vision deteriorated due to the heavy studies. He then moved to the other German-speaking region, Germany. He settled in Wehrmsdorf, where he raised a substantial family.

The Budan Home in Wehrmsdorf

The students of the Gymnasia, European high schools of that day, knew how to write and communicate in Latin. At that time, in the late 19th century, it was not a dead language. It was the means of communication (Latin) that later on my father and my grandfather used to correspond.

During the outbreak of World War I and the entry of the United States into the war, my father did not have a difficult choice because the central powers, Germany, Austria, and Turkey were allies. Of course, Turkey was a red flag for any Macedonian. For that and other reasons, he joined the U.S. army. He was wounded during the 1918 conflict. However, he had no animosity toward the Germans or the Austrians because during his experience, they had been helpful to him.

2

Historical Review

This summation of the events leading up to my internment is designed to give a full synopsis. World War I came to an end as the result of President Wilson's Fourteen Points which included many issues, such as the notion that peoples of a race and language would be together and there was also the issue that there would be fair play. On the basis of the Fourteen Points, Field Marshal V. Hindenburg recommended to the German Emperor that Germany surrender on those conditions, which they did. The German Navy sailed to Scapa Flow, where it eventually was scuttled by German sailors. The German Navy was on strike, i.e., a mutiny, following the Battle of Jutland or the Skagerrak 2Schlacht, depending upon which side of the fence you were on. That was the end of the German High Seas Fleet.

The postwar era saw competition between patriotic groups in Germany and the left radical communists. As a result of wartime Germany, the National Socialists group evolved with the notion that the Jews and the Communists were of the same ilk and had committed treason. The fury of the German population was directed against both the Jews and Communists. Both the Jews and the Communists found ready acceptance in Concentration Camps.

Hitler came to power in 1933, and the annexation of the Rhineland followed, as well as the annexation of Sudetenland on the Czechoslovakian border. In 1938, Germany annexed Austria. All these steps found great support from the German population. I had grown up in this climate, and I felt that the German position at that time was correct. The problem was that as the War came to be in 1939, things went array. The collapse of the Polish Army was followed by the German invasion of both Norway and Denmark. The reason was the Germans felt the British were ready to move into Norway and outflank them. Then, the Germans invaded the Netherlands, Belgium and France. Benito Mussolini, without much consultation with Berlin, had entered the fracas coming across the Alps into France. The notion was that Mussolini wanted to be in on the Peace Treaty, which everybody thought was about to occur. Field Marshal Petain of France was ready to work with the Germans to establish a new order in Europe.

I had, because of my interest in horses and equestrian parts, volunteered to the Waffen SS, Division Fegelein. General Hermann Fegelein was a renowned horseman. He did not have much luck, though. His wife was the sister of Eva Braun, later on to become Hitler's wife. When things started to collapse in Berlin, he was caught in civilian clothes and was summarily executed.

After my 16th birthday in August of 1944, I was called to the German Draft Board. At that point in time, I was scheduled to be inducted into the German Army. The Germans at that time had a system where they had a Wehrpass, a passport designating the troops and units to which a person was assigned. When it came to that, I insisted, that my regarding Wehrpass state I would not be used against American troops under any condition. Why? It is because my brother was in the United States, presumably in the US Army, which he was, and serving in the Pacific. He was on the Corregidor and was a participant in the Bataan Death March, which is another story. The German official at the Draft Board ridiculed me and said that I would probably need some reeducation in a Concentration Camp. When my mother heard that, she instantly communicated with the Swiss Legation in Leipzig demanding that I be interned as an American citizen, which I was. (see chapter 4)

In many ways I suppose this German official did me a favor. If I had been with Fegelein in his Calvary Division in the Eastern Front, I probably would not have survived the War. That's another story and we will never know.

The Richardson Family,
Left to right: Florence, Tommy, my father, me and my mother

My first years in Germany

My mother went through what the Germans called a Handelsschule where she, in addition to typing, became fluent in English, French, and Spanish. This schooling would eventually prompt her to return to Germany because during the Depression, there was a lack of opportunity for someone in the United States who did not have advanced U.S. training.

Before he met my mother, my father was previously married to a lady of the Earp Clan from St. James, Missouri. They had produced two children, my brother Tom and my sister Florence. However, my father's first wife died during childbirth. Because of the horrendous German inflation and the associated economic problems in the aftermath of World War I, my mother emigrated to the United States in the meantime with the hopes, that things would be better. And, they were. Her uncles in St. Louis gave her a base from which she moved forward. It was in St. Louis where my mother and father met. They were married. They moved to Minneapolis, where my father was the proprietor of a beauty and barber salon.

Then, I was born in 1928. Soon thereafter the economy of the U.S. entered the Great Depression. In 1935, my grandfather in Germany passed away and a new phase of my life began.

In 1935 on the occasion of my grandfather's death in Germany, my mother and I undertook a trip while the U.S. was in the midst of the Great Depression. Fortunately, when we arrived in Germany, they had a terrific upswing, economically speaking. People were at work. Maybe not doing what they would like to do, but they were working.

When we came back to the United States, my mother and father separated. In 1936 my mother gave me a choice, either I get a pony or we go to Germany. I was adventurous, and we moved to Germany.

The German perception of the U.S. was very positive. That was because the United States did not ratify the Versailles Treaty, and the Germans felt that they had been wronged by it. So, there we were! In 1936, the Olympics were in Berlin. There was a fellow by the name of Jesse Owens who caught the imagination of everybody in Germany, in the United States, and all over the world. Even Adolf Hitler invited him to come to a private reception.

While I was there, I attended school. The vacation scene was over, and I didn't speak a word of German.

I went to a public school initially in the Hoepkestrasse when I was 8 years old, and I was assigned to the class of Mr. Engel. He lived a few blocks from the school.

He would invite students to come to his home where we would have a wonderful time. The problem was that I still did not speak German well enough to compete. My mother enrolled me in the private school of Dr. Wiener one year later.

I stayed there until it had to close. The reason for the closure was that teachers were being drafted. There just weren't enough classrooms available. 1942, I transferred to the Annenschule, a Real Gymnasium.

The Vice Director of that school, Dr. Forberger, was a patron of mine. He saw to it that I got into the classes that I needed. Believe it or not, that school covered ages 10 through 18.

Dr. Forberger   Dr. and Mrs. Forberger

We had all kinds of good teachers:

Dr. Forberger taught German, Dr. Kluge Latin. My English teacher, by coincidence, had once had my mother in his class! Then, there was "Gandhi", which was a nickname. The reason he was called Gandhi was because he looked like Mahatma Gandhi. He taught math, calculus and science as well. When not in the classroom, he was a skilled mountaineer. Then, there was the music teacher. We students had nicknamed him "Schwein" (pig). The reason he was called that is because when the National Socialists came to power, he divorced his Jewish wife, took her property, and sent her packing. Kids are pretty observant about these events. We just did not think he was a gentleman.

When I entered the class, there were 44 of us. When I left, only 16 remained.

4

Consequences of war

I had a problem with bronchitis when I was living in Germany. We moved out of the Elbe Valley to the healthier town of Klotzsche, which was up on a hillside. Today there is a major airport there.

I took my ten riding lessons at the Tattersal in Dresden. There was an organization called "Jung Volk" for ages 10 to 14, a part of a younger Hitler Youth. Initially, I was introduced as a guest. The leader of that group was Fähnleinführer, Heinz Finger. He happened to be a neighbor who lived a few houses down the street. We became good friends. He was drafted and served in the submarines. The first time on leave, he was very enthusiastic. The second time he was depressed. He did not come back a third time.

My stay at the Tattersal, where I had ten riding lessons, came to an end because the horses were drafted. For that reason, I tried to get into the Hitler Youth when I was 14 years old. A Gefolgschaftsführer, Heinz Krieger, endorsed me. The reason was he figured that anyone who paid for ten lessons, and then had the horses drafted from under him, couldn't be all bad.

The Gefolgschaft consisted of approximately 200 boys. There were four levels, age 14, 15, 16, and 17-18. There were 28 horses and four carriages or coaches. The boys had to do all the work, feed and care for the horses, and attend to civil air defense.

During such night duties, I slept on a simple bunk bed; I turned out the light— . . . tip, tip, tip little feet walked across my chest. I jumped up, turned on the lights, and barn rats scurried into their "dwellings". Needless to say, I left the lights on!

Periodically, a ratter would come by the barn. We would open the door to the stable, and the ratters (dogs) had a field day killing rats. The dogs would grab the rat by the neck; shake it, thus breaking the neck. These night outings cost the lives of 16-18 rats each time.

As the war progressed, the various Gefolgschaftsführer, Krieger, Ranft, among them, were all drafted. The Equestrian Hitler Youth boys had to attend classes on horses. I saw to it that the horse was the theme of our Wednesday meetings. There is a saying in German which goes like this, "Das Glück der Erde liegt auf dem Rücken der Pferde". What does that mean? "Happiness on Earth sits on the back of a horse." If and when one wanted to ride, one had to show equestrian proficiencies. We rode out in the Dresdener Heide.

Each time when a formation came to a close, a ritual followed. The opening statement would be: "To the Victorious German Troops", and then all 150 boys would chant in unison the response, "Sieg Heil, Sieg Heil, Sieg Heil."

What it implies is that the German troops are victorious. Afterwards, the formations are dismissed. Everybody goes home, turns on the radio, and listens to the news. "German troops have successfully moved into new positions in the rear." That means they had to retreat. A feeling of gloom permeated the atmosphere. The Youth was determined to help change the direction in which the War was going, refusing to accept the superiority of material on the side of the allies. This was a key factor in grinding the German forces into the ground.

Progress in the German high school was quite difficult for me. My mother had seen to it that I had subsequent private support in order to keep up with the math program, calculus, and all the other programs. She engaged a graduate student from the Technical High School in Dresden. He was engineer, and that was very helpful. She also engaged Professor Gebhardt to help me with my Latin and German literature. He was quite a gentleman and a friend of Dr. Forberger. Between them, they saw to it that I made progress.

In 1943, my mother secured enough flour and other food stamps so that she could engage a baker to prepare several sheets of Streuselkuchen. This is a cake that is about 1-1/2" thick with streusel on top. This cake was for my confirmation.

My 1943 Confirmation
From L Rear to Right:
Mr. Gunther, Onkel Rudi Schuvig, my aunt Elfriede, his wife,
Aunt Irmgard Budan, Yours Truly, my uncle Hans (in uniform) in front
of Mr. Gunther, aunt Erika, my mother, cousin Klaus
Front left: Sieglinde and cousin Eva, and two neighbor children.

My uncle and godparent came. Johannes Budan received Army leave to come to Dresden for that occasion. He was, I believe at that time, in Greece where he had been with the German Quartermasters.

During 1943, the Germans had reasonable control over their railroad lines and highways. They even had some connections to the Romanian oil fields. Things were, for the German civilian population, bearable. However, after that and especially in 1944, things went from bad to worse.

Hermann Göring, the World War I German Ace and the Luftwaffe Leader, had promised the German people that if the Allies took control of the air space in Germany, his name henceforth would be Meyer. Well, Meyer had a problem. The American British Air Forces had secured absolute superiority over Europe. The Germans had some very good airplanes and some outstanding pilots. The problem was that they didn't have, from their point of view, enough. From our point of view, things were going just fine. The National Socialists propaganda machine kept insisting that retaliation weaponry was in the process of being introduced into the warfare. Indeed, some of that stuff started coming into play; the V1 rockets and the V2 rockets. Believe it or not, the Germans were the first to introduce jet airplanes in combat. The problem Germans always had was while they had high quality equipment, they never had enough of it. Another big hole in their armament routine was that they lacked fuel. Synthetic gasoline and the little oil that came forth from Romania was not enough to change the scales in the battles that ensued.

In the fall of 1944, my mother and I found that there was a real problem, even though we all had Ration Tickets. The German Transport System couldn't get supplies to the various stores, and there were many, many empty shelves. Now and then, we would get skimmed milk and a few eggs from the dairy stores. Bread was a crude mixture of wheat, sawdust, sugar beets, and other substances that were mixed into the flour so that you would have some loaves of bread. Potatoes were the staple. My mother and I went up the Elbe River and tried to secure food from the farmers who were supposed to deliver to the public stores and collection agencies. But because of the disruption in transportation, they never quite could.

I was the mule or burrow or the beast of burden—I had to carry this stuff! We went to the farmers and we purchased potatoes, sugar beets, carrots, turnips, and many food supplies that one could store in the cellars without refrigeration.

Totally exhausted, we would arrive home and put these supplies into the cellar space where we would keep coal for cooking and heating. Now and then, my mother had good luck and she would purchase six or eight eggs. They, too, were in short supply.

In those days, the Germans took the view that if you did not contribute to the war effort, you would not eat as well as those who did. The best cared for were the Americans, and that had nothing to do with our contribution to the German war effort. It had something to do with the reciprocity of the way we treated Germans, and the way they treated us. The Brits were next in the good graces. The worst off were the Russians. They did indeed have to work, and they worked their butts off. In the end what choices did they have?

If they were liberated by the Russian Forces, they surely would be sent to Siberia because the Russians did not think that they would be henceforth reliable. The French and the Yugoslavs were sort of in between, as were the Poles. The Poles, the French, and the Yugoslavs tended to work on German farms. For them, that was good because there they sat right where the food was. Although, they did not get fat, in the end they had something to eat.

The military situations were not going well for Germany. The Russians had succeeded in driving the Germans out of much of East Prussia. They were at the eastern frontier of the old Germany. The allied U.S. and British forces had succeeded in landing in Normandy and were moving forward. In France, General Patton was making his swift and bold strikes toward the so-called Siegfried Line.

In Germany, and in their desperation, they were starting to draft 16 to 65-year olds into their forces (Volkssturm). As a leader of the Hitler

Youth, I was presumed to be in charge of 150 boys in my Gefolgschaft. I took military training with the Waffen SS Pioneers in the vicinity of the Dresdener Heller.

The main event for me was that we ate some really good food. I also enjoyed the exhilaration of firing some machine guns. Every one of the boys was a pretty good marksman with rifles, having practiced with 22s, and standard German Army rifles. How to use a machine gun had to be learned because one had to train oneself <u>not</u> to keep one's finger on the trigger because the Machine Gun 43 could fire 2,000 rounds a minute. Too long a burst meant that you had to carry more ammunition with attendant difficulties. Also, I learned to use a Panzerfaust or Bazooka. We also gained some knowledge on tank warfare. When you see a tank on film, it looks impressive. But, when you stand next to one of these things, heaven help you!

The noncoms also showed us what would happen if you did not dig your foxhole deep enough! Those mean tanks, the Russian T-34s, could spin their tracks over the hole. If you didn't watch out, they would and could do you in!

5

Draft and internment

When I turned 16, along with other 16-year olds, I was called before the German Draft Board chaired by a Colonel seated directly at a table in front of us. We all had been medically approved. This Colonel with his staff was at the table. At the far end of the room was a group of Waffen SS officers. The Colonel said, "You all have been approved and you will now be sworn in as soldiers of the German Army. If there is anyone present who has any reservations, let him speak now." With that invitation, I spoke up. I said, "I am an American citizen. Before the war, my mother and I belonged to the American Church in Dresden and attended the various American functions. We were in Germany on an American passport. I would not bear arms against the United States."

That was a little dumbfounding to the Colonel. I added that I would consider that if my Wehrpass, the army document that German soldiers carried with them, would stipulate that I would not be used in Front Services, on the Western Front, or against American troops, I would be ready to fight the Bolsheviks in the East. The Colonel said, "We don't make exceptions. You are either in or you are out. I think you are going to have to go through a concentration camp reorientation program". I was a little dumbfounded. It was even dumbfounding to the German boys who were with me on that occasion. Germany surely had enough volunteers who were fighting against the Soviet Army and they were not Germans. They were British and French. There was a Spanish Division. There were Latvians and Estonians. The Germans even had Cossacks in their Armed Forces. I decided that keeping my big mouth shut was probably at that point in time the best thing. I reported to my mother what had happened, and she instantly communicated with our Swiss protectors in Leipzig. The Swiss Consular Services in Germany looked after the interests of American citizens. They demanded that I be interned according to the Geneva Convention. I was then programmed to go to Spitall and later to Laufen.

The SS Officers who were at my induction said nothing. A few days afterwards, one of the officers came to my home to discuss the situation with my mother saying that that Colonel was way out of line. Of course, everybody knew that the German troops were full of foreign volunteers. There was even a Palestinian brigade sponsored by the Mufti of Jerusalem. My mother informed him that we had initiated steps with the Swiss Consulate in Leipzig and that I was now being processed to be interned.

The SS Officer, according to my mother as I was not there, paused for a long time, and then added, "Madame, we have lost the war.

Your son is a fine young man; let him be interned. Our cause is lost". With that he thanked my mother, and she thanked him. He left. It was obvious by then with the Soviets moving on to Berlin and the onset of the Battle of the Bulge that things were coming to an end.

In January 1945, a nice 65-year old gentleman soldier carrying a rifle and his rucksack came to escort me, an enemy hostile, to Spitall. As we were approaching Regensburg on the German railroad, the train that we were on was hit by a strafing attack. We all got out of the train and moved along the tracks trying to get to the other side of Regensburg, where another train had been made ready to take us onto Munich and into Austria. As we passed one railroad passenger car, the door was open, and there was a decorated German soldier sitting smoking a cigarette. My guard said, "Comrade, aren't you going to come out and take cover." The German soldier just turned and spit out the door and said, "Comrade, I am sitting here dry and clean. If I go out, I'm going to be dirty and wet, and if it is going to get me, I am going to be gotten while I am dry and clean." We got the message and we moved on. He stayed there. We never knew what happened to him.

Eventually, the transit to Spitall concluded. Attitudes of various German commandants were quite evident and different. The German Commander of that camp in Spitall had lost his family in a Berlin air raid. Contrary to the Geneva Convention, he did not allow us to take cover during air raids. On the other hand, my campmates were largely Australians and New Zealanders and a better group of men you could not have found. They had been captured by the Germans when their ships were sunk and they were Merchant Marines.

I had barely settled into the camp for about a week, when I received a communication that I had been selected for a prisoner exchange program. I would have to be transferred to another camp in Bavaria near the township of Laufen. Across the Salzach River was the church in Oberndorf where the Christmas carol, "Silent Night, Holy Night", had been written. The transfer took place forthwith.

I will never forget my Australian and New Zealander campmates. They had made a regular sport of going into the mountains to cut trees for the Germans, and then ride them down the hillside and make their short-lived escapes.

The Germans, at that particular point in time, had a habit of yelling three times, "Halt, halt, halt." The next sound you heard would have been a "bang" when they would be shooting at you.

Just about that time, the German High Command issued the following corrective measure. It was posted and announced to all prisoners in these various camps.

"The German High Command no longer has any sympathy for the sport of American, Canadian, Australian, and New Zealand prisoners in making escapes." For that reason, German guards have been instructed that if anyone of us allied prisoners tried to escape, they were to yell "Halt" once and simultaneously shoot. I have to say that slowed our escape efforts down.

Two days later I arrived in Laufen, and that was a totally different camp. We all felt sorry for our German Commander. He was a German Reserve Officer who had immigrated to the United States after WWI and worked in Detroit as an engineer in the automotive industry. In 1939, he came back to Germany to visit his parents. Alas, the war broke out, and he was back in the German Army as an officer. He was a gentleman, and he saw to it that we were properly treated. The American Commander or Senior Prisoner was Samuel Gompers, Jr., son of the AFL President, Sam Gompers. He did not go back to the U.S. with us. He married a German lady in Laufen.

Sam Gompers Jr.

Most of the prisoners in the camp where I was were largely of Polish American background, and British. We also had a Mountbatten who was a hostage from the British side. There was also a Polish General Boer who led the Warsaw Uprising.

What do you do when you are in a prisoner of war camp? You try to get as much physical exercise as you can. I initially started to learn boxing with a British middleweight champion, Billy Bennett. He was champion of the British Channel Islands. But, my friends in the camp told me, "George, Billy is still fighting the way they did in the last century." I said, "Oh?" They said, "Yes. Look over there. Do you see that guy?" I said, "Yes, I see him."

"That's Joe Kowalski who is the Polish heavyweight champion. He fought Sharkey. He fought Schmeling. He didn't win against Schmeling, but he fought him.

Gompers (left front) Joe Kowalski (right rear)

Take your boxing lessons from him." And, I did. Joe Kowalski was one of my role models for the rest of the war and my athletic life. His brother was with the Free Polish Government in London; what a group of people.

Another individual in our camp was Mr. Stoyanovich. He was in charge of distributing the American Red Cross packages. I can only say one thing. Hooray for the American Red Cross!

We Americans had the best Red Cross distribution system in the Prisoner of War camps throughout the war. We received each week a Red Cross package containing cigarettes, chocolate, coffee, tea, Oleo margarine, and Spam. To me that was a feast getting Spam. Now, I guess a lot of people would say why would you consider that a feast? Well, it is when you have no meat.

What the Germans gave us was soup and a few slices of bread, enough to keep the body from turning into a cadaver. But, with these Red Cross packages, we were leading the life of Riley, and Riley wasn't even in our camp.

Later on when Sam Gompers, following the British-American air raids on Dresden, insisted that my mother be interned in Liebenau near Lake Constance, things were indeed coming to a close. The good news for my mother was that the camp in Liebenau was in a Roman Catholic Monastery, and the nuns were looking after the internees. That is how my mother eventually survived the war because following that bombardment in February of 1945, I do not think any Americans or British would have been treated with kid gloves by the German population.

As 1945 came to a close, the atmosphere in Europe was one of fear. People were afraid; they were afraid of bombardments, afraid of persecution by one side or by the other side. My uncle, who had been at my Confirmation, had been in the meantime moved up in rank to Colonel. But, as the Germans withdrew from Greece, they had to fight their way back to Germany, and my uncle was wounded. He ended up in a German field hospital. He was liberated, whatever that word meant, in Sarajevo by Tito's Partisans and Yugoslavs. In addition to his wounds, he also suffered from dysentery. Indeed, my mother's packages to him, as well as to other relatives, saved their lives.

My cousin Eva and her mother did not survive the Soviet Liberation. Their grandmother took the two boys, Klaus and Hartmut, on the terrible trek from Selasia, where they had owned a farm, into the refugee camps, fortunately in Western Occupied zones. That is how they survived. My aunts and their friends managed to eke out survival.

In all of this, my mother was totally engaged in supplying them with packages so that they could survive. They had food with which to trade. Those were difficult times.

6
End of the war

As the war came toward an end, it was in May after Hitler's suicide on April 30th 1945, the German Waffen SS Division of Adolf Hitler was withdrawing across the Salzach Bridge toward Berchtesgaden, where they had anticipated making a last stand. The SS Officers came into the camp and demanded from our German Camp Commander that he turn over the hostages, like the Mountbatten and Boer, and the Americans, of course. The German Commander said, "No."

The German Commander then summoned the British and American Room Elders because we were about 10 to 12 people in each room and told us the following. He said, "American Forces are less than a hundred miles away and they are moving rapidly toward Laufen." He added, "I have ordered our machine gun towers to turn their weapons around. Instead of facing in toward the inside of the camp, they are now faced out. I have ordered that the armory be open to you Americans and British. In case the SS insist that they want to come and get you, you defend yourself." We will never forget that man. The German Master Sergeant, who was in charge of the German enlisted men, ran toward the armory and said, "I will teach you how to use these weapons." That wasn't a big deal. Everybody in that camp knew how to use the standard German military rifle and light machine guns.

Then on May 8th, there were no more German troops to be seen anywhere. The guards on the towers had disappeared. The gate opened to our camp, which was a 14th century fortress or monastery, whichever you prefer, and a Sherman tank stood there. For me, that was the end of the war. I discovered that the Hungarian Army was demobilizing so I drove some of their carriage horses—after all, I loved horses!

About five or six days later, American Consular Officers came and interviewed us. Within a few days, I was on a plane (a DC-3) flying from Salzburg to Paris. I have to say that plane was full of shrapnel holes and pretty well "air-conditioned"! But, we did get to Paris.

When we arrived in Paris, no one seemed to know we were coming. That was typical of the U.S. Armed Forces at that particular point in time, especially when there was a changeover from Supreme Headquarters European Forces to the EUCOM (European Command).

So, what did I do? I became a Black Marketer! The GIs weren't allowed to go on the Black Market and sell cigarettes and the like to the residents of France, but there was nothing stopping me from doing that! As a result of all that, I ended up having a profit of a couple of hundred dollars in American currency in the end.

So much so, that when we arrived in New York and the American Red Cross asked my mother if we needed money to get back to Minnesota-Wisconsin, my mother said, "No, we have money."

7

In memory of Tommy Earp

I had a wonderful half-brother, Tommy Earp. He is the son of my father and his first wife, who died in childbirth. Tommy became the adopted son of his maternal grandparents, the Earps.

He was expected to inherit the farm. World War II set him on a different course.

Tommy as child

Tommy G. Earp

The St. James Leader newspaper in St. James, Missouri published the following article dated September 9, 1943. **"2 Local Boys Reported Safe in Jap Prison Camp."** "Relatives of Tommy Earp and Daddy Burns Receive Post Cards." The article then reads as follows:

"Two St. James boys, Japanese prisoners of war in the Philippines, are both reported to be alive and well, according to post cards received here by their parents from the Japanese government through the International Red Cross and the War Department.

"They are: **Sgt. Albert "Daddy" Burns, foster son of Mrs. J. C. Burton; and "Pvt. Thomas "Tommy" G. Earp, son of Mr. and Mrs. W. T. Earp.**

"Their relatives received the cards Sunday morning, and it was the first word heard from the boys since they were reported captured several months ago. They were both stationed at Manila, P. I., when the Japs struck. The cards were brief and to the point, and the only identification as to their handwriting was in their signatures. The rest of the message were printed or typed. Sgt. Burns was reported to be interned in the "Philippine Military Prison Camp No. 8"; and Pvt. Earp in "Philippine Military Camp No. 2".

"Pvt. Earp's card ran like this:
"IMPERIAL JAPANESE ARMY

"1. I am interned at 'Philippine Military Prison Camp No. 2.'
"2. My health is—excellent; good; fair; poor. (The word "good" was underlined.)
"3. I am—injured; sick in hospital; under treatment; not under treatment. (The latter phrase was underlined.)
"4. I am—improving; not improving; better; well. (The last word was underlined).
"5. Please see that 'Mother' is taken care of.
"6. (RE: Family): "Best of love and send this to dad and sister."
"7. Please give my best regards to "Florence and Dad.""

Tommy Earp, as a prisoner of the Japanese, survived the Bataan Death March. Toward the end of World War II, the Japanese evacuated the Philippines.

The Japanese were not signatories to the Geneva Convention. The ship my brother was on, therefore, had no Red Cross Markings. It was sunk.

Another newspaper article followed:

"REGIMENT WIPED OUT ON BATAAN TO BE REORGANIZED"

"New Thirty-first Infantry to Have Original Trophy Buried on Corregidor.

"TOKYO, Dec. 27 (AP)—Wiped out on Bataan in 1942, the Thirty-first Infantry Regiment is to live again.

"Gen. Douglas MacArthur announced today the new Thirty-first will be organized in Korea about Jan. 19 and attached to the Seventh Division, replacing the homeward bound 184th Regiment.

"The Thirty-first will have new colors and guidons to replace those burned on Corregidor, where a few survivors made their way after the valiant stand on Bataan. The regiment will have its original silver punchbowl trophy, made from 1500 Chinese silver dollars and buried on Corregidor before the Japanese arrived.

"Survivors of the original outfit now serving in the southwest Pacific who wish to return to the Thirty-first will be transferred to Korea. Headquarters said there was no official estimate as to their number, but that it was negligible.

"The Thirty-first is the only unit of the United States Army which never served in the United States. It was activated originally in the Philippines and remained in the Orient."

8

From Paris to the U.S.

There is an interesting episode during our stay in Le Havre. The Americans were strongly advised against going out at night into the city of Le Havre because the French population was not too happy with us. They said, "When the Germans came, they didn't destroy our town. When you Americans came, you flattened the city." I do not think that went down too well.

My mother joined up with us fellows in Le Havre, Camp Home Run. We went from Le Havre to New York on troop transports. We had to sign an I.O.U. for being taken and brought back to the U.S. Boy, I tell you there was nobody happier to get out of Europe than my mother and I.

Unfortunately, we had rough seas when we were leaving the English Channel and going into the North Atlantic. Talk about a ship full of seasick soldiers! The soldiers had originally placed themselves on the deck. But, because of the heavy seas, everybody was ordered below deck and got properly seasick. Talk about a stinking ship! Aye, aye, there was puke all over the place. So much so that when we pulled into the docks of New York, people tended to back away.

The first to disembark were the soldiers. At last, it was our turn to get off this vessel. The American Red Cross again was there. I can only give them my compliments.

I really don't know how we would have fared had they not been there and taken charge. They are a wonderful group.

9

Visit to Neillsville, Wisconsin

The Red Cross sent a number of communications to friends we had throughout the country in order to give us a starting base when we tried to spread our wings. The first to respond were Drs. Milton and Sara Rosecrans of Neillsville, Wisconsin. While the American Red Cross told the folks that both my mother and I were in good health, there was a certain amount of scepticism inasmuch as the American wartime propaganda apparatus showed all these terrible pictures and stories coming forth from the prison camps in Europe.

My mother and I were placed on a train to Chicago and on to Neillsville, Wisconsin. In travelling through the peaceful country and the farmlands, one could not imagine that we had just left the war-torn areas of burned-out cities, destroyed towns and buildings, and masses of refugees. When we arrived in Neillsville, the Rosecrans family was indeed very happy to welcome us. Drs. Rosecrans, both of them were MDs, had two daughters. One was Elizabeth Ann, she was closer to me in age, and we had been good friends before the war. Then, there was Laura Lee, the younger daughter.

We started in a more working relationship. Believe it or not, I had to go to school! It was August and school started in September. I lived across the street from Coach Hollie, our football coach. He was operating a little small dairy business on the side. Any able-bodied boy in a smaller country school was fair game to be on a team. That was good for me because I immediately had contact with boys of my age.

Back Row: D. Anderson, C. Swensen, J. VanTatenhove, B. Madsen, B. Seif, E. Wagner, R. Schultz, W. Elmhorst, B. Stucki, T. Casler
2nd Row: Coach Hovey, Mgr. R. Klann, B. Larson, R. Connverse, R. Jenni, D. Trewartha, B. Harder, R. Schultz, D. Patey, E. Ott, H. Blackhawk, Mgr. E. Wall, Asst. Coach Ruedy.
1st Row: M. Tock, F. Zilk, R. Eggimen, R. Pscheidt, B. Farrand, G. Richardson, C. Dierrcks, R. Stanley, R. Cummings, D. Mattson

#81 with Neillsville Football Team

One did in effect have good relationships so that when I entered the school, I was not the outsider anymore. I was part of the team. I don't remember how well we did, but I know that we traveled to many different towns in the state. It was a great experience.

However, in the meantime, my mother wanted to make a permanent transition to the Twin Cities. When my mother's girlfriend, Mrs. Donlin passed away, her apartment became available through the OPA (Official Price Authority) and other housing controls that were in effect during that time. We found ourselves very fortunate to "inherit" her apartment on Dayton Avenue in St. Paul. We moved to St. Paul, and I was enrolled at the Central High School in St. Paul.

John Donlin, my boyhood friend and the son of Mrs. Donlin, came by for a brief visit. He was already in the service (Navy) and our relationship cooled.

On the other hand, he had a cousin. That lady and I dated a few times. The biggest story is that when I entered Central High School in St. Paul, again, the American Red Cross used me as a bulletin board card for their good works during the war.

I came from Germany where boys and girls went to separate schools. A coed situation was a new experience for me. Believe it or not, it was something that I had to get used to! The young lady, who lived a few houses down the street from me on Dayton Avenue, Elizabeth Montgomery, offered to teach me how to dance! Social dancing—the two-step. Whoopee! I was going up in the world! This was again totally new to me! The Germans had a saying "Errötend folgt er ihren Spuren und ist von ihrem Gruß beglückt." Blushingly, he followed her footsteps and was delighted by her greeting and recognition.

There were a number of coincidences, such as being Protestant. We went to a Lutheran Church on Marshall Avenue. Obviously, I went to a school in the attendance area and the Church was in the school's attendance area. Then, there was Bud Nelson. Bud Nelson had a sister by the name of Joan. I never dated Joan, but boy did I have a crush on her. There was also Charlotte Relph. She found out that I liked to go horseback riding, and she coaxed me into joining the Horseback Riding Club. In this way I became introduced into the social life of an American high school.

As far as the academics were concerned, they were less challenging than what I had experienced in Germany. I had to take U.S. History because that was a required course for graduating. I had to take Civics and English. Most of the other subjects in the curriculum were a review of what I already had in Germany in the schools in the Gymnasium that I had attended. So, academically it was a soft ride. Socially, I had to get used to the fact that there were girls in the class. Now and then I would go horseback riding. There was the Minneapolis Park Riding Academy that was owned by Mrs. Paul. They were all good horse people. Mrs. Paul married Mr. Nordquist.

One day they asked me if I would mind giving riding lessons and taking the groups out on the trail around the Lake of the Isles and a number of other locations. My first chance to make some money, and I accepted! From that point forward, I suppose I was a professional. Colonel Donohue liked what I was doing. He was the owner of the Minneapolis Park Riding Grounds, and he had gaited horses. I was with my true love for horses again! Life went on.

Finally, I graduated from Central High. There was a discussion that my mother and I had about me attending a University. My mother thought she could fund it. I didn't think she could because we had lots of relatives and friends in Germany who were in dire need of the packages which my mother sent in care of the Pastor, who confirmed me, and to others.

She did not indicate in the covering note who she was, so Pastor Oertel responded to Mr. or Mrs. Richardson. It had not dawned on Oertel who my mother really was.

I saw clearly that I could, by enlisting in the U.S. Army at that point in time, get in on the GI Bill of Rights, and with a three-year enlistment, secure four years of University credits. So, that's what I did.

I went from St. Paul via Fort Snelling outside of Minneapolis to Fort Riley in Kansas during a rainy season. That was an interesting experience because when it rains, Kansas is a very muddy establishment. In Kansas, I was questioned about which branches of the service I would like to be in. There I made it clear that with my linguistic qualifications, it would be natural for me to be in counterintelligence, and that is eventually what happened. But, I had to go through basic training. For that, I was sent to Camp Lee, Virginia outside of St. Petersburg. After successfully completing my basic training, I was transferred to the Holabird

Signal Depot (the CIC Training Center), just outside of Baltimore in Maryland.

Specialagent, CIC

I reported to the Holabird Signal Depot, which was the training center for prospective counterintelligence agents. We had a joke going in Holabird. If you took a Japanese course, i.e., the Japanese Language Course, you would surely end up in Germany. The other version was that if you took German, it would be inevitable that you would be assigned to a detachment in Japan. Neither turned out to be correct. We were trained in German or Japanese languages. We were trained in the methods of sabotage, self-defense, the silent kill, and every other thing that an agent would need to be a master of on his various assignments. Duty was duty and then there was free time.

The USO provided many opportunities for dating. My favorite date turned out to be Dotty Crockett who lived at the time on Guernion in Baltimore. She was a Miss Maryland in 1947. However, all these wonderful things, such as my training in Baltimore came to an end. I departed from Camp Kilmer to Bremerhaven then to Marburg.

Marburg was the Collection Center from which American personnel were being assigned to the different locations in occupied Germany. While I was in Marburg, I met a very fine young lady, Margaret Kaiser. We were good friends, but nothing serious.

I was assigned to the 427th CIC Detachment that was then located in Heidelberg. I reported to my Commander, 1st Lt. Cormier, a real Intelligence person, a French Canadian by birth. He had been in the OSS and had worked behind the German lines in France, and had lost a finger there handling explosives. He and I became good friends. Later, when I married, he served as Best Man. His wife, the daughter of an Indian British Brigadier, helped with the wedding preparations.

CIC Agent, George Richardson

Because of my linguistic expertise in German, I was given the assignment of screening all non-American personnel who were assigned to the U.S. Constabulary Forces of Germany. I was also given other assignments. One of these assignments was the security for General White, the Commander of U.S. Constabulary.

The First Ball at the University of Heidelberg staged in 1947 was sponsored by the Chancellors of the Law School and the Medical Faculty. General White was guest of honor and stayed for about a half hour. Then his MPs came and he was driven off. All this happened in the Grand Ballroom in the Heidelberg Castle. After General White had left, the German MC came by to see if it was all right for Germans, i.e. "indigenous persons" to be seated at the General's table and at my table. There were only four people at my table, and the tables accommodated twelve. I asked whom he had in mind and he pointed to a group of students standing in the doorway. There was one young lady there especially who instantly took my fancy. She had laryngitis and couldn't speak a word. However, I did learn from her friend, Rosemary, her family history.

Hildburg 1948

The next day, "by chance", I came to her school. I said a friendly hello and how coincidental it was that having just met her the night before in the Heidelberg Castle that I should have met her there. I asked if I could give her a lift. She said she was going into Heidelberg to the Bauamtsgasse. I said, "Well, I think we'll find it if you will just give me proper directions." Of course, I had known where she lived. Needless to say, I drove her home and that was the start of something that turned out to be the best thing in my life.

10

Heidelberg

While I was in Heidelberg, I didn't waste my time just chasing girls. Instead, I took up fencing. My teacher was Gaston Hamory. He was a former Hungarian Lieutenant Colonel. He was also a member of the former Hungarian Polo Team, and they were European Champions. He was an expert fencer in saber, épéé and foil and had been on Hungary's National Team. Needless to say, I enjoyed these activities very much.

Author on Butterball in Heidelberg

There was also horseback riding. My regular mount was Butterball, but I did get to ride the Blue Danube and other top German Olympic horses. This experience sharpened my equestrian skills. It also became acquainted with Eric Bubbel, who later came to the United States and worked in Santa Barbara for the then Retired General White. He was always a fantastic horseman. I think his endorsement where he stipulated that my equestrian skills were such that I would not have any problems finding work with leading equestrian establishments. This carried weight, when I applied for permission to get married.

Just about this time, I received my "Dear John" or "Dear George" letter from Greta, a girlfriend in Los Angeles, in which she told me that she was engaged to somebody else. That ended that. I was really upset. In those days, Counter Intelligence Agents could just hop on a plane.

We were always armed; I had a Smith and Wesson 38. Our credentials enabled us to pretty well go anywhere. My CO was Captain Gutterman. He wisely took my 38 from me, my credentials, and grounded me. About a week later, he called me into his office and said, "George, aren't you dating that German girl, Hildburg, whom you met at the Castle?" I said, "Yes, I am." He said, "Do you know that she is taking riding lessons, and she is paying for them? She is trying to impress you! And, here you are moping about something that has long passed. Go and make out with that young lady and forget about your ex-girlfriend in Los Angeles." I said, "Yes, Sir!" I trotted off, and lo and behold, soon confirmed that Hildburg was taking riding lessons. The instructor had only three horses. That was all he could afford. But, the girl i.e. Hildburg was indeed learning to ride and taking to the horses quite well. I was impressed. Needless to say, there were many dates that followed.

In the spring of 1948, we were still chasing down the so-called "Nazi Leadership". Most of our apprehension of big-named National Socialites came to us by means of informants. We had large networks of informants that helped the CIC locate a number of individuals that we eventually did arrest. There was a captain of Adolf Hitler's personal bodyguards who was still on the loose. We had a lead that he was and could be located near Mannheim, not too far from Heidelberg.

Often SS individuals had really only a few choices; either they were lucky enough to skip and skedaddle into France or Spain and going from there on occasion to Argentina if they had connections there.

This gentleman, and I use this word carefully because he was a gentleman, was surprised by Lipinski and myself. As it was in the evening, he asked us the favor if it would be all right for him to have a parting dinner with his family and fiancé. Lipinski wasn't so sure but then the man added, "You have my word of honor that I will not make an attempt to escape." With that having been said, and we looked at the man, both Lipinski and I knew that we had a man whose word was his bond.

Lipinski and I sat in the living room while his family was having their farewell dinner. The SS Captain asked me what he should pack for his stay in Dachau. I told him, "Well, you're going to be spending a lot of time in a not too pleasant environment, so have something that can take the wear and tear. But, when you have your day in Court, have something so that your appearance is as solid as it is when you are standing here in front of me."

He thanked us for the information, turned around and left. While Lipinski and I were sitting in the living room, Lipiniski was second guessing himself. Then, we heard crystal glasses klink and chime. About fifteen minutes later, our Captain stood there ready to go.

I never heard what had happened to him. But, I had asked him, "Look, it's just between you and me. Is there anything that they can hang on you where the Israelis, the Jews, might be mad at you, or that the Russkies could get after you?" He said, "No." Again, I took him by his word, and I said, "I think you'll do all right in Dachau. It may take a while, but you'll do all right." That was one episode that I will never quite forget.

Another episode was when Lipinski and I again received tip-offs from informants who told us where we could locate General Streich. Streich was never quite a name that his erstwhile boss had. He was Chief of Staff under Erwin Rommel, a Field Marshall. After Rommel's death, Streich was put in charge of the German Reserve Armies. That was quite a joke because they were drafting 16-year olds and 65-year olds. Anybody who could hold a rifle was being whisked into the German Army. It was a hopeless case. Everybody knew it except Adolf Hitler! Toward the end, he did realize it, and to quote from Linge, his valet and personal adjutant, "When some of these SS Generals wanted to have that last stand in Bavaria near Berchtesgaden, Hitler said, 'No, that would no longer be appropriate!'"

The thing that the German upper hierarchy was looking for was someone the Soviets and the Western Allies could negotiate with, if you want to use the term negotiate, but it wasn't much of a negotiation, because the Americans, the British, and the Free French, and the Russians insisted on unconditional surrender. Most of the old field marshals didn't quite want to buy that, but they had no choice by that time. They did after a while get down to Admiral Dönitz, who had achieved a degree of notoriety as Chief of the German Submarine Fleet. It was he who at the end signed the unconditional surrender documents at Rheims.

An interesting postscript, after and when Dönitz had died of natural causes (he had been tried as a war criminal, but he was set free) many former German Naval Officers, including my later brother-in-law, Fritz Bernd, were quite upset that this honorable person in fact was not given a military funeral.

Getting back to General Streich, again he was a gentleman, when we addressed him by name, he said, "Yes, I am he." The only thing I can say to that is that Counter Intelligence apprehended him, secured him, but we were not in on the debriefing of such a relatively high-ranking individual. MI and G2 were in charge of General Streich and that was the last I saw and heard of the gentleman. And, he was a gentleman.

Our detachment was transferred to Stuttgart in Baden Württemberg. My assignments basically were the same. Now and then we would do security checks of headquarter buildings where we found many things were amiss. But, we always set them straight. On one of these occasions, I met a German informant who told me about the Soviet uranium mines in East Germany. The Soviets caught on to him, and I saw to it that he and his family escaped and came into the Western Zones where I also assisted him in finding work. I had a feeling he was quite grateful.

He said he had nothing with which he could show his gratitude. I said, "Well, your handshake is enough for me." He said, "No." He had salvaged a porcelain stagecoach, which I still have. Those were the hardships that many people were experiencing in the divided Germany.

The porcelain stagecoach

I also started the system in the Counter-Intelligence Corp where, as a hangover from World War II, many people were preoccupied with hunting down Nazis. I was more preoccupied with ferreting out Soviet spies in our military apparatus. So, it was that the daughter of one of the Communist leaders in Heidelberg was dating an American sergeant. Indeed, they had infiltrated our Signal Depot. We put a stop to that.

There is another incident that somehow sticks in the back of my mind. I had a very good friend, a MP, who often drove me around. Eighty percent of the time I was in civilian clothes.

As it was and as it turned out, we had a real problem with black marketeers stealing American motor vehicles. I was assigned on one occasion to the area where they were dismantling and stripping the vehicles. I was up there on a hillside stakeout, when they arrived. I put the floodlights on and said, "Halt or I'll shoot!" They started running. I had an automatic. It went "click, click, click" but not "bang, bang, bang". These guys ran right past me so close that I could have hit them over the head with the pistol. From that point on, I never carried an automatic. I only carried 38-caliber revolvers. Now that 60 years have passed, I am kind of glad I didn't shoot them because I couldn't have missed, and they would have been dead. My MP friend did not have such good luck.

He came upon the motor vehicle thieves as they were in the process of ripping off some jeeps. He fired one shot and killed one man. The others stopped. The poor guy kept asking me, "Did I do the right thing?" I assured him, "You did what you had to do."

My MP friend who had to shoot a car thief.

Privately, I was thinking that this was something he was going to have to live with. There is something different when you kill a person eyeball to eyeball than when you face a combatant whom you don't know at a greater distance across the trenches.

Proposal to Hildburg

I finally proposed to Hildburg, and she accepted. We set up an appointment to inform her father of this. I did not have the feeling that he was that keen about us getting married because the U.S. was a long way from Germany. However Hildburg said to him, as I told by my late sister-in-law, Carmen, she is going to marry me whether he likes it or not. She is of age, and that was that. Having said that, my father-in-law finally gave his blessings.

At this time Hildburg's father was a freelance economic and finance adviser. After the first World War he worked as a manager at the department of Oldenburg. In the years from 1923 to 1933 he had been a county administrator.

After that he became the director of the "Landeselektrizitätsverbandes Weser-Ems", until 1945 he was president of the "Energieversorgung Weser-Ems".

At the end of the war he was discharged, but then the British called him back in to get the Northwest German Power and Water System going, which he did before he retired. Then, Adenauer called him back into service to get the West German Railroad out of the red and get it functioning again, which he did. After that, he again retired. But, then Chancellor Erhard called my father-in-law back to lead the German Economic Commission to Rome and Brussels where they established the European Economic Community with the Treaty of Rome. Then, they moved the EWG to Brussels. In later years when my father-in-law came to visit, he had a diplomatic passport and was a VIP. Washington was very interested in whom he was contacting with while in the U.S.

Hildburg and I did get married in Stuttgart on March 11[th,] 1949 at a Civil Service, which by law is required in Germany. Two weeks later we were married in the Catholic Church in Kornwestheim. The Cormiers and Captain Gutterman were my witnesses for the civil service. Hildburg's best friend from Kindergarten on, Rosemary Roepke, then Husted, and her then fiancé, a cousin of Hildburg, Bernard Kronerabe, were witnesses in our church wedding in Kornwestheim. We went on our honeymoon trip paid for by black market cigarettes. I was skilled in that trading business. We went to Freudenstadt in the Black Forest and we stayed at Hotel Waldlust.

Hildburg and George are married, march 11, 1949

Our detachment occupied the residence and villa that belonged to the Salamander Shoe Manufacturer, where I had a fantastic room. Now, that I was married, we had to get an apartment. My comrades in the CIC made sure that we had everything we needed. There couldn't have been a better relationship. In this transition, if you will, there was one fellow who had to make a serious adjustment. That was my Rottweiler, my dog, Harras.

Author and his Rottweiler,
Harras vom Jakobsbrunnen

He was a fantastic creature. He was initially jealous. I didn't blame him because instead of him sleeping on my bed, he now had to sleep at the foot of the bed. In the end, Harras stayed with my in-laws in Oldenburg. Later, Hildburg obviously followed me to the United States.

In 1949, we had winter maneuvers in Southern Germany. It was coordinated with the French and British Forces and, obviously, the Constabulary Forces representing the United States. The Constabulary was an armored cavalry division. I came down with what I thought was a cold, and it turned out that I had pneumonia, followed by asthma. I was not able to get time off or go on sick leave, or go to the hospital because I had to be in the field as a linguist and interpreter between the German community, the French, and the Brits. All of this worked out fine because when the maneuvers were over, I was in the hospital sick as a dog, and my dog was staying at our apartment with Hildburg! Finally, the doctor came and said, "Young man, you are not fit for military service any longer." I said, "Oh." He said, "No. I am going to put you on a hospital shipment back to the U.S."

Then, he gave me a list of potential locations that would be appropriate for me. He assigned me to Letterman General Hospital in San Francisco.

I was initially transferred to Bremen where I was hospitalized. My father-in-law came and visited me. Hildburg came and visited me. Come to think of it, my German relatives all came and visited me. Only my dog couldn't come. For some reason, we Americans have a lopsided relationship when it comes to dogs.

But, my father-in-law assured me that Harras was welcome in their home. He stayed with them until he died of old age or natural causes.

My father-in-law was very proper. He saw to it that Hildburg had a dowry. The Quartermaster Crew packed it and shipped it to my father's home in Los Angeles on Juliet Street. We said our goodbyes, and we were on our way. It was not exactly the way I thought I would be going back, but there I was on a ship, comfortable with white linen. Really, it was not bad! Once in the U.S., I was placed on a hospital train. I traveled all across the United States. I found Battle Mountain in Nevada was especially impressive. Why? Because, there were horses near the railroad!

I arrived in San Francisco at the Letterman General Hospital. Finally, the doctor said that there really wasn't anything that they could do. They would prescribe medications, and I would be given an honorable discharge. All this transpired. I got my discharge, went to a clothing store, and got my first real civilian suit. I got on a Greyhound Bus and traveled to Los Angeles where my mother was happy to see me. My father said, "Son, you are welcome." Hildburg came a few weeks later, and we started our life in Los Angeles and the United States.

As a closing statement, March 11th, 1949 remains for me the happiest day of my life, and I have no regrets. Hildburg and I had a wonderful life.

We also had our trials and tribulations, but much of it was bridged by our love for each other, for our horses, and later for our dogs.

Father-in-Law Accomplishments

As the war came to an end, Hildburg's home, that is my father-in-law's house, was hit by a 500-pound bomb. The two upper floors had been destroyed. My father-in-law was not too happy about that, but then he saw the bright side of it. He was assured that there would be no way that the British were going to take his home and billet troops in it! So, after a number of years the outer walls to my father-in-law's house were rebuilt. The inner walls and the appointments were not. The roof was put back on and in that way he avoided having British troops billeted in his home.

Because of the bombing that Hildburg's parent's house had experienced, Hildburg's father moved his family to relatives out into the countryside, thinking that would be the safer place, and thus avoid bombs. In some ways it was true; no bombs fell there, only Canadian troops came through as they were moving into Northern Germany. Hildburg and her sister, Carmen, were with some of their relatives. As the fighting raged between German troops and Canadian troops, the Germans withdrew along the canals in that region.

One thing has to be noted. Both Hildburg and her sister, Carmen, spoke English. When the Canadians pulled into the farmhouse and the

German population who was in the cellars came out, Hildburg felt that she and her sister were very lucky. The Canadians quickly realized that improper conduct on their part could easily be reported to the British command by the English-speaking sisters.

The Canadians were there for a while. Hildburg, her sister, and their relatives were put into another area of the farm. Finally, the Canadians moved on following the retreating German troops. When Hildburg and her sister went back downstairs into the basement of the farmhouse, they discovered all of their family jewelry had been swiped by the Canadians. All I can say is that Hildburg's mother (she was a Baroness before she married my father-in-law) had an awful lot of jewelry. As a result, poor little Hildburg still had some jewels when she and I got married.

The von Twickel Estate in Holland, Hildburg and her parents

Hildburgs grandfather Baron von Twickel

Those are the fortunes of war. The good news was that being able to speak English spared Hildburg and her sister the experience of rape. The bad news was that they did lose some expensive jewelry. That was the only close call Hildburg and her sister experienced. War does strange things.

The survival of war is often a question of luck. Hildburg's two brothers, Fritz Bernd and Juergen, served in the German Navy. I don't remember which one of them, but one of them was a very good friend of Meinrad von Hohenzollern-Siegmaringen.

It probably didn't hurt that the Jahnstrasse 7, my in-law's address in Oldenburg, was also the home of two very good-looking daughters, Hildburg and Carmen. So, it became a hangout. I did have the opportunity to kind of reminisce about war's fortune or lack of it. Hildburg's younger brother, Juergen, was a Naval Bridge Officer on the cruiser "Medusa". That cruiser was anchored in Wilhelmshaven and was packed with anti-aircraft guns. While on a leave or pass, Juergen was absent from his normal station on the bridge of the Medusa. The person who took his place took a direct hit and was killed. Hildburg's eldest brother had a number of naval commands in the North Sea. Toward the end of the war, Fritz Bernd was given the command of a German ship in the Adriatic Sea. That ship's task was to resupply the various German fortifications along the Coast of the Adriatic. What was not so reassuring was that each of his two predecessors had been killed in action, i.e., their ship was blown up from under them. Fritz Bernd was lucky. He took command of his vessel and sailed the Adriatic, and the war ended. What Fritz Bernd did was turn his ship over to the American officers in Trieste. He became a Prisoner of War, which is a lot better than being blown up.

The Brand Family. Left to right
father Friedrich, Fritz-Bernd, Jürgen, mother Maria-Antonia,
Carmen, Hildburg

The third of these three young lieutenants, Meinrad von Hohenzollern-Siegmaringen, was an officer in the German Navy.

He was kind of hanging out in Oldenburg until he felt he could return to Siegmaringen in Southern Germany. I met him and others on a number of occasions. He quipped and said, "George, you are the only American that I have ever met who speaks English with a Saxon accent." The Saxon accent was not a very popular accent in Northern Germany. I don't know why, come to think of it. A lot of people in Germany, who used the German Saxon accent, were very prominent in German history. I am not talking about the more recent history. At any rate, this too ended.

13

Life in Los Angeles

Once I was in Los Angeles, like any good American ex-soldier would do, I bought a blue 1939 Chevrolet coupe for $900.

Hildburg at the pacific coast, '39 Chevy

It was the first car Hildburg and I owned! It was then high time for us to hurry back to Minneapolis because I wanted to register at the

University of Minnesota where my mother's lawyer, Mr. Thompson, felt I would have a good chance, especially with the funding from the GI bill. The problem was that by the time we got there, the registration had closed. I had to scramble to make some money.

I went back to the Minneapolis Park Riding Academy. Obviously, my position had long since disappeared. But, I did get a few days of hard work. Hildburg and I were debating what to do next. I guess there was a divine intervention.

Hildburg came down with pneumonia because of a tremendous temperature shift. She also had a problem with asthma, as well. She looked me in the eye and said, "George, please take me back to California where we belong." It made sense. We packed our car, and we were on our way back to California.

My father had a very large house. He put us in a room with a bath and made it available for us. We stayed there and I enrolled in USC.

Hildburg in front of father's house with sister Florence

We started out on a $105 GI allotment which didn't seem to cover very much then, even in 1949.

I was, in fact, successful in getting a position as Riding Master and Instructor at the Sleepy Hollow Riding Academy. My riding classes numbered somewhere between 70 to 100 students. Obviously, I was not sitting on a horse, but I was using a PA system. In all respect to the horses, I think the horses paid more attention to me than to the riders, because when I said "walk", they'd walk. When I said "tttttrrrrot", they would trot. When I said "prepare to canter", their ears perked up, and then when I added "canter" they went into a slow canter. Horses are wonderful creatures. They can be easily spooked, but I love them dearly.

While I was at the Sleepy Hollow, the horse business started to fade somewhat in the Los Angeles area. I then followed up on a lead where the Beverly Hills Saddle Club was asking for a riding instructor. I drove out there. It was not in Beverly Hills, but it was on the Brentwood Polo Grounds. Al Murabito was the owner along with his wife, Dottie. He was a great guy. I asked him if he wanted to see me ride or anything. He said, "No, no, no. If you can do it where you were at, you can do it here as well." So, I ended up being the Riding Master, not just at the Beverly Hills Saddle Club, where I had Marymount School and Westlake School for Girls as riding students, but I also had a number of so-called VIPs.

Al Murabito and author

George on Brentwood Polo Grounds

Burt Lancaster took some riding lessons from me. Betty Hutton had her kids came.

The problem there was that she had just worked on the "Greatest Show on Earth" and C. B. De Mille gave her a pony for her kids.

Parents, if you ever come across this, please keep one thing in mind. No Shetland pony for your kids. Shetland ponies are strong, strong-willed, and especially the circus horses that were from a Liberty Act. Every time, I would raise my hand, he would get up on his hind legs front feet off the ground, and "plop" there went the little kiddies. The pony was okay in harness, but I think it did more harm by dampening the youngsters' enthusiasm for riding.

Among my students were Frank Capra's daughter, Lucille, and her horse Maddie. There were a number of extremely well-known people from the Hollywood crowd such as Dawn Adams. Lana Turner's daughter was one of my students. It was a fantastic operation.

Time-wise, it worked out. During my morning hours, I was at USC trying to learn something. In the afternoon I was with the horses. In the evening, I was still at Sleepy Hollow instructing these very large classes. You have to keep in mind that the patrons, or customers, at the Sleepy Hollow were paying $2.50. I got a dollar out of each transaction. It was quite a bit of money back in the 1950s.

One day we all got the sad news that the Los Angeles Athletic Club had sold the polo grounds on which stood the Beverly Hills Saddle Club.

The sale was for the purpose of building a high school, a junior high school, and other school facilities. That was the end of that episode.

Directly across from the Beverly Hills Saddle Club, was Captain Egan's stable. There were a few customers who were somehow taken because where do you go when you have no place to put your horses? Among them was Elizabeth Taylor who had a big Sorrel over there. Captain Egan and I agreed to transfer the willing customers to the Dincara Stock Farm in Burbank where Jack Deneen was the proprietor.

These events shortened my revenue and things at USC were not moving as well. I was probably doing a year's worth of academic progress in two years' time. I was more interested in earning money for current use than an academic project for extending one's earnings at a later date. I therefore used my experience from the CIC. First, I was a private detective for Stewart and Lame, and also for Pinkerton Detective Agency. Those were sporadic jobs and of limited dependability.

Then, I "enlisted" into the LAPD, Los Angeles Police Department. I went to the Police Academy. For me it was a perfect situation. One thing that I had not calculated on was that they had an Internal Affairs Division, and they had a grim view of police officers having outside income. I did have an outside income because I was servicing my customers from the Beverly Hills Saddle Club, Westlake and Marymount.

The Internal Affairs Department said to me, "Either you are a Policeman, or you go with the horses." The joke was that the LAPD would have withheld any funds that I had placed in the LAPD Retirement Fund. That would be an outright loss. So, either I cut my ropes then, or the pain would come later. I resigned from the LAPD.

I made a transition to the Golden State Dairy Company and became a milkman. I did that for about a year and a half.

My business was such that I was at the dairy between two and three in the morning, loaded my truck and made my deliveries by ten in the morning. In the afternoon, I was free to continue giving riding lessons.

One of my friends was Jack Connors. In motion pictures he was known as Jack Carry, and he had a problem. They were making a big western in Mexico and there for all the equestrian stuntmen were in Mexico. Columbia Picture was shooting a picture locally in the Los Angeles area in Chatsworth called "Indian Uprising". The scene was when George Montgomery, as leader of the Cavalry Troop, was cornered by an Indian band and had taken shelter underneath a fallen tree. So, all three of us, Jack Carry, Doug Gunther, and I became the mean Indians who rode over George Montgomery. We also rode over the people who were shooting at us. Yes, they were shooting blanks, but horses don't like it when it goes "bang, bang" in front of them. So, they needed a few strong riders. And, that is where we came in.

Jack Carry, Doug Gunther and Author

At the end of the day for that day's work, I received $250. The production manager came up to me as we were settling our account. He asked, "Do you fall off a horse?" "No, I stay on pretty well", I said. He added, "We pay $100 to $150 if you fall off a horse". I said, "I will fall off a horse for you for $100 to $150!" And, that is how the stuntman, George Richardson, came into being.

Author doing saddle fall

I worked on many pictures. One of them was "Trackdown". We all wondered how Robert Culp was going to carry the show. He did a good job of it. Then Four Star produced another show, "Wanted Dead or Alive". They came out with a new acting star, Steve McQueen. I doubled for Steve McQueen and did a horse fall for him. What in the world is a "horse fall"? That is when the horse falls and plays dead. Steve liked that horse (Woody/Firewood) and I liked him, too.

Author doing a horse fall

He was my horse, and he was a registered thoroughbred. He had a fantastic gait. Steve wanted Dick Powell, who was one of the four owners of Four Star Productions, along with Charles Boyer, David Niven, and Ida Lupino to buy my horse.

Woody asking, if it is OK to get up now

I went to Dick Crow who was the gaffer. The gaffer is the person who runs the horse commitments for Four Star. I said, "Dick, don't let them buy the horse. I mean it is tough for me not to say "no", but they are going to blame you and me if that horse kills Steve." Steve had a lot of guts but he was not a good horseman at that time. He developed some skill as time went by, but at that time the horse would have killed him. The other thing is that Four Star and Warner Bros. would ring a bell when they got ready to shoot. When you ring a bell, your thoroughbred that had been on a race track would be ready to run! That was Woody's favorite moment of excitement. Woody was the falling horse.

Anyway, Steve did not get that horse. I made quite a few pictures for Four Star. Jack Sonntag and Frank Bauer were my supporters at Four Star. It was a successful monetary boost for me.

Then, along came Elvis Presley. Elvis Presley was an unknown. He had just come out with a number of rock and roll songs. I was on a motion picture for 20th Century Fox called, "The Far North". All of us stuntmen were pulled off this because Elvis Presley's song "Love Me

Tender" had an earlier release than had been expected and that was the name of the picture.

So, we were put on the second unit. The second unit was the action unit. There is not much drama or acting going on there. There were a lot of "bang, bang" and galloping horses, and people falling off horses and hanging up in their stirrups, horses falling, and horses jumping over barricades. It was a Civil War story with Richard Eagan and Debra Paget. They were shooting in such a hurry. Instead of what normally would have been the practice of agreeing beforehand what you were going to be paid for a given stunt, the production manager just came up and asked, "What do we owe you?" They did not want any disputes because that film was being released two weeks later. Some of the best action scenes were left on the cutting room floor because the film had to get to the theater. The song, "Love Me Tender" was a knockout.

Subsequently, I worked on a few Elvis Presley pictures. As far as I know, he was a very fine gentleman. He did have a bunch of what I called "hanger-on-ers", which was a sort of group of six or eight people who were always around him. I never could see what purpose they had other than keeping Elvis happy.

Stanley Steamer going over a wall Stanley Steamer going over jump

Four Star, 20th Century, Columbia, Disney were all studios where I made enough money to pay off my home, my vehicles, and finally I was able to return to USC. This time, I did not go on the GI bill and so I had to pay tuition with my money. Compared to what they are paying now, that was really very little. In January of 1962, I finished my studies at USC and received a Bachelor of Arts in International Relations and Economics.

Universities have a weird sense of making money—they sell "units". I was excused from physical education and many other activities because of my military service, but boy did I have to take a lot of units! I enjoyed being outside, so I took up the Birds of California and I was spending time down in Malibu watching birds. That wasn't the worst activity and I still got credit.

I did enjoy my fencing experience with Colonel Hamory when I was in Heidelberg. For that reason, I took up fencing at USC. The Fencing Master at USC was Gene Hermans. He had been Belgian champion, and he was also in the Berlin Olympiad.

He also worked at the Motion Picture Studios when they were doing a number of those fencing movies, Cyrano de Bergerac, Scaramouche, and a number of others. The motion pictures always wanted a wild swinging sword wielding hero. That was far from reality! Gene Hermans had a difficult time persuading the Motion Picture Studios to get a true understanding of how fencing worked, both in foil, épéé, and saber. They are not the big moves. If somebody were to come at me swinging a sword the way they do in the motion pictures most of the time, I would surely have scored. The moves in fencing are very refined, doublés, cutovers, small moves, foil, or sword tips and trying to get the access or the entrée so that one can move into score. Obviously, each of these three disciplines in fencing had different targets.

When I was at USC, I took the classes that Gene Hermans gave. When you are in a class, you can also join the Fencing Club at USC. When you are in the Fencing Club, you are on the Fencing Team. Among other things, we did fence against the LA Athletic Club. Here, I have to note one thing. In fencing women and men are equals. A woman can score just as well against a man as a man against a woman. Mrs. Bauer at the LA Athletic Club was an extremely outstanding fencer. That is one thing in fencing you do not lose with age. Any woman, who has an interest in athletics, should consider fencing. After a fencing bout, even though I considered myself quite fit, I often found myself lathered in perspiration.

You do not see the big moves, but those fine moves, those advances, those retreats, those little moves with your wrists and forearms are extremely demanding.

So much so were Hildburg and I involved in fencing that I purchased for her, as well as for myself our own fencing masks, jackets, gloves, and foils. We practiced fencing at home. Fencing is another love. Unfortunately, you cannot do everything. Hildburg and I had to let it pass in time.

In 1962 after I had graduated from USC, my father-in-law invited us to come to Germany, where he had quite a few friends.

Among them was Dr. Bergemann, who was head of the Margarine Union in Germany which is a British-Dutch conglomerate (Uni-Lever) specializing in margarine, fish, and plant oils. I was interviewed, and I was accepted to be the assistant to the Professor, Dr. Schuethauff, who had had the Chair of the Economics Department at the University of Kiel. When it was my turn to ask questions, I asked them why they were interested in me? Dr. Bergemann and Dr. Schuethauff reminded me that my age group in Germany had been wiped out in World War II. In other words, it was a demographic factor that propelled them to offer me this promising position. Hildburg and I accepted on the condition that it would be a trial year.

The nice thing about it was that Hamburg has an outstanding equestrian center. There, I was able to renew my love for horses. There were also opportunities to ride in Oldenburg, Hildburg's hometown. This all made my stay very comfortable. However, Hildburg and I never quite got used to our outsider status. Hildburg's girlfriends would tell her it would cost ten marks to have a dress altered. When she got there, it was 20 marks! In other words, when we opened our mouths we were right away pegged as Americans and the prices went up!

Prior to leaving for Germany, I had been offered an internship by USC to enter into the teaching profession in California. The internships would have been with the Los Angeles School System. Hildburg and I agreed that that would probably be for us expatriates the smartest thing to do. So, we reluctantly informed my father-in-law that we were going to terminate my contract with Uni-Lever. My mother-in-law didn't speak to me for probably another year because Hildburg was obviously following me back to the United States. Carmen understood, but Carmen's husband who was an extremely successful businessman in Germany said, "George, you're crazy.", as did my other brother-in-law, Juergen, who wrote me several letters stating that I should reconsider.

Hildburg and I made our move back to California. Obviously, I instantly went back to work. When I came to the Studios, they would say, "George, where have you been? We haven't seen you in a while!" The standard answer in Hollywood was, "I have been working." What they naturally would assume is that I had been working at the Studios. Again, things worked out. I did my student teaching, my internship and I received an opportunity as a regular teacher at Los Angeles High School on Olympic Boulevard. It was a school of 3,600 students at that time. The Harrison Family, or "Harrison money," had put extra funds into the ASB (Associated Student Body) budget.

It was a good school. It was integrated. At the time when I entered, there were about 30% Black and 20% Asian. Nonetheless, we had a fantastic staff and everything was going well. My initial Principal was Mr. Holt. Later on, the man who helped me make the big transition to Administration was Norman Schachter. He was the NFL football referee who didn't know that after two comes three, not four. Evidently, they missed a down in one of the professional football games. I was in the office and had to take the telephone calls from all over the country that reminded me to tell Norm Schachter that he should take some remedial math's so that he would not forget that it is 1st down, 2nd down, and then 3rd down before you get to 4th down. Well, that too passed. Norm Schachter in my mind is a fantastic person.

While it is the habit when you are in the education business to take additional courses, I discovered that I was very close to a Master's Degree in Education. If I took the right courses, I would have a Master's Degree in School Administration and School Supervision. Well, I did that! That was during my fourth year of teaching. Norm Schachter discovered that near the corner where my classroom was, there were never any students clowning around. The students had somehow developed a respect for that ex-stuntman who was in a classroom there. Then, Schachter made me Boys Adjustment Coordinator, which meant that I had to hound the halls and get the kids into class. The bad boys had to be assigned detention. Or, if they were caught smoking or doing other mischievous things like smoking pot or selling drugs, then they were suspended. These are duties that I assumed. For some reason, when some of the kids said, "Mr. Richardson, won't you please give me some slack?" I would come back to them and I would say, "If I give you slack, then I would have to give everybody else who is similarly situated and sitting in the chair that you are in the same kind of benevolence." Kids understood that. A couple of times, some kids tried to run away. There was a 12 foot chain link fence and a gate. The gate was closed, two kids ran out, and they scrambled up the fence thinking that they had evaded capture, only to find that I was right up there with them! They said, "Mr. Richardson, you are too cool!" They came back down. We went to the office and they took their punishment with "good grace."

I had however come to realize that as former State Superintendent, Riley had once said, "There are two kinds of administrators, those who are location-bound and those who are career-bound. Location-bound administrators tend to stay in one community.

Career-bound administrators go wherever the job offers them opportunities." I elected in part because of my age to be among the latter. I saw an ad through USC from Arcadia. This was during the time when we had all sorts of student unrest on the various universities and high school campuses. I put in an application.

I had that first leg up as Boys Adjustment Coordinator at Los Angeles High School. I didn't think that I would get any response because Arcadia was a highly rated school. For somebody to get an Assistant Principal assignment there, it would be a big plum. Lo and behold, during one of the rioting days when there was a fire on the stage at Los Angeles High, a visiting delegation from Arcadia came. I thought, "Oh, oh, there goes my chance." Anyway, I was the only administrator on campus, and I had to put out the fire. The injured students were taken to the Nurse's Office. I had corralled a bunch of students who were sitting in my office waiting to be suspended. It was really not so often that the local students were the problem. It was more likely that interlopers came onto the school and created mischief and egged on students to do things that were not appropriate.

As I was doing what I had to do, I had very little time to even say hello to Elb Sauders and Dick Cordano and other members of that Arcadia committee because I was too busy. After about an hour of them roaming around on L.A. High campus grounds, they came by my office, and they said, "Mr. Richardson, I think we've seen enough. We will be in touch with you." With that, they left.

A few days later, we had another altercation on campus. We had an outstanding Chinese science teacher. There was a certain amount of rowdiness going on at campus. This was coincidental to the Watts Riots. I was on grounds supervision at lunch time. I didn't know it at the time, but it was a group of these outsiders who came on campus where I intercepted them. I said, "Gentlemen, with the provisions of Ed. Code 626, I have to ask you to please leave the campus. You are trespassing." These guys stood in front of me and they sneered at me and they said, "Who's going to make us?" Before I could really say anything, there were about two dozen guys in blue letterman jackets. They were known as the "Big LA". That was the veteran LA High Football Team that later almost in unison moved to USC. They came up behind me. I think it was Reggie who said, "You heard the man. You're leaving!" These interlopers looked at each other and then looked at these lettermen. There wasn't one who was under 6'5" and 200 pounds, at least. The interlopers then said, "Okay, okay, we're leaving." And, they left.

I went back to the office, enrolled a new student, and that little idiot went outside where there was a group of individuals hanging out. Before anything could be done, he was swamped and beaten up. I had to call the nurse and the boy was eventually taken to the hospital. I had to arrange for him to go to another school.

Juan Carenga was on the other side of Olympic Boulevard in front of the public library. Juan Carenga was a Black Panther, a leading activist in the Black community.

I went over to him and there were hundreds of people standing around him, and they were not LA High students. I asked, "What is your problem here?" He said, "We want more Black people here." I said, "Well, wait a minute. Hold the phone. Do you know that this kind of ludicrous behavior is not going to attract good teachers to our campus?" He took a long pause, then I added before he could respond, "One of the teachers who had just started last week, a Chinese science teacher, walked into the Principal's office, threw his roll book on the Principal's desk saying 'I came here to teach, not to engage in combat.'" Juan Carenga looked at me and said something to the effect, "You're right.", and he told his followers, "Let's clear out." These were difficult times. It was especially a difficult time for the various school systems that were going through the integration processes.

There was also the problem associated with the expectations of being in a first-class school like Los Angeles High School, which was at that time one of two prestigious schools, the other being Fairfax. The expectation was that somehow by osmosis, success would come to these young people. It doesn't work that way. You have to work for it.

Arcadia High

The following school year I started my work at Arcadia High School. Arcadia High School was having its problems, too. Student unrest, student expectations, classroom boycotts, and just plain old horsing around. These kids were influenced by the commotion in Berkeley, because Arcadia was one of the top schools in Los Angeles County. Many of their graduates would go on to Berkeley, which is still a top university in California. Arcadia was a turning point in my career.

Dick Cordano is a very special person. He became a role model for me throughout my time in education and in the years that followed. I was introduced to the high school clerical staff, including my new secretary, Mrs. Unbedacht, and the man I was replacing, Richard Caroll. I discovered that Richard Caroll had an interest in sailing, too. So, it turned out to be a very cordial and pleasant transition. I was in charge of the Athletic Program, AFS (American Field Services), and many of the clubs. I was also in charge of school discipline. All of these duties kept me rather busy as the school year progressed. That particular year and through the years that followed, Arcadia High School had an outstanding football team. Many of those students went on to USC and other top universities. When you are winning, it is a happy school. But, when you were losing, it was not so good.

We also had a fantastic marching band. Ron Hoar was in charge. He was also in charge of the Pasadena City College Band. Arcadia was and is still an outstanding high school.

At the time when I joined Arcadia, I would say that 95 percent of the student population was White. As I understand it, it is now nearly 95 percent Asian. Either way, the academic excellence and the accomplishments of the students cannot be put in question. Dick Salter was a highly-skilled football coach. He and I remained good friends throughout the years even after I left Arcadia. There was also the Athletic Director, Dave Ackerman, another good friend. One of the things that was disturbing to the community in Arcadia was that the football uniforms were sort of tattered and of the Knute Rockne variety.

Dick Salter and I orchestrated a program whereby parents and members of the community would sponsor a student, or more, to work in the foothills of the National Forest in a Weed Abatement Program. Thousands of dollars were brought in, it didn't hurt that the Spanjian Family had students in our high school. A year later and by the time the Arcadia football students came out on the field, they were all in brand new spanking uniforms.

That does lift the morale of the players. It was a very successful football season. I think we won the CIF for our section.

Doug Smith was the school's track coach. If one thought that the football players of old looked sort of plain, the Track Team was in rags! Doug Smith asked me if we couldn't do the same thing for the Track Team that we did for the Football Team. I said, "Yes. I think we can." Some of my experiences in staging horse shows and equestrian events didn't hurt either.

We had a bicycle marathon. There were about 80 to 100 students on the Track Team. Each student went out to get sponsors. The sponsors pledged donations for how many miles or rounds on the Track Field these kids were able to do. Lo and behold, with the next track season, we had brand new uniforms. And, again, those new uniforms helped. We probably had the best dressed Track Team around. It also coincided with the time that the Arcadia Invitational Track Meet came into being. School spirit was really running high.

Arcadia High School 2013

15

Borrego Springs

In my consultations with the Educational Placement Office at USC, I learned that either one is location-bound and satisfied with the success one has, or one is career-bound and then gets on the treadmill and marches to wherever there are job opportunities. Arcadia was a settled, firm, and fantastic community to work in. However, I elected to get on the career-bound route, and applied here, there, and everywhere for an assignment as Principal. Eventually, I did get one with the Borrego Springs Unified School District. Borrego Springs at that time was expecting a curriculum accreditation review. The reputation of Arcadia as a curriculum standard bearer didn't hurt me when I applied at Borrego Springs, and I was selected to be the Principal of that school. That opportunity exposed me to not just high school and other school situations, but at times I also had to fill in as acting Elementary School Principal. In addition I had to take charge of the Special Programs, such as School Improvement, E.I.A., Limited English Language Programs, and Title I. This kind of experience eventually led to my return to the so-called big city.

Borrego Springs was a very unique community. I was once asked during an interview for another position, "If one were to go to a large district or a small district, where does the student do better?" I unequivocally answered, "In the small district." There each student was known and the teacher paid more particular and personal attention to the individual. In Borrego, a school of 250 students, we had an excellent coach, Coach Souza. We had eleven-man football teams. This reminded me somewhat of my experience in Neillsville. Any boy who had pants on was pretty well guaranteed to be a member of the team! We had the usual ups and downs, some losses, wins, and ties. We also played a Mexican high school. On that occasion our band had to play the Mexican National Anthem and the American National Anthem. Could you imagine that some of the football players had to switch to play the musical instruments in the band at the opening and half time ceremonies? That was a terrific experience. Even years later when I went back to Borrego, I saw Reno Hartman. He was the ASB President at the time when I was there. The kids seemed to remain in the Valley. Others went onto Berkeley or Stanford where they became lawyers, engineers, and doctors. We had an enviable cross section of academic and individual talent among the students in Borrego Springs.

16

Back to Los Angeles and ABC

Superintendent John Prieskorn eventually ran into some difficulties. The Board was not too keen on any of us three administrators who were on salary, Eddy Eickart, John Prieskorn and I. Eddy became Superintendent at the Calipatria Unified School District, and I returned to the big city. There was one smart thing that I did when I went to Borrego. My wife and I did not sell our home and our property in Glendale, California. Believe it or not, I was back in the Motion Picture Business periodically. My former coworkers did not know where I had been. They asked me, "George, where have you been? We missed you!" I said, "I've been working". And that was not a lie!

After I had received my doctorate, Dr. Edward Bobier and Dr. Rasmussen secured the position of Associate Professor for the University of San Francisco for me. The University had an extension program in Los Angeles County and there were quite a number of graduate students who were seeking to receive a Master's degree and an Administrative Credential. As an Associate Professor, I taught a course that was entitled, "School and Community". In the urban areas of California and especially in Los Angeles County at that time, we had an influx of new populations.

They were not just American Indians, but they were also Asians, Koreans, Vietnamese and others. These populations required opportunities to participate on Parent Advisory Groups so that a meaningful instructional program could be developed for their children in American high schools. Dr. Bobier unfortunately had a heart seizure and passed away while this course was in progress. As a matter of fact, his demise occurred in the first week of that program. It fell upon me to teach both his section and my own section.

I am very happy to say that there were many, many students who reached their goal of a Master's degree and an Administrative Credential and who were able to apply this new learning to their professional careers. One particular individual who comes to mind is Jeffrey Green. He not only finished these courses and got his degrees but soon after finishing this work, he moved from being Principal of a junior high school to Principal of Cerritos High School, a larger school in Los Angeles County. Jeff Green is a personal friend of mine, and I was happy to see his career progress. At any rate, all is well that ends well.

Eventually, I did connect with the ABC Unified School District where I had a short stint as a School Disciplinarian. I guess they pegged me as being able to keep the school discipline going.

The ABC Unified School District was facing two problems. The first problem was that they were in need of money, what school district isn't? And, they were also facing a District accreditation review. So, when the Personnel Office elected to give me a March 15th pink slip, one of the Assistant Superintendents, Charlie Ledbetter said, "Wait a minute. You can't do that! He has a Ph. D. That is important in accreditation situations." So my March 15th letter was rescinded and I stayed with ABC where I took over the specially-funded school improvement Title I, EIA, and LEP and also the American Indian Education Program. We had quite a few Indians in the ABC School District. My exposure to international situations in my earlier years stood me in good stead for my work at the ABC School District.

Indian Education Program

While with the ABC Unified School District, I had this Indian Education Program. Included in the program was consultation with the Parent Advisory Committee in the Education Programs. This led to the need to conduct cultural enrichment experiences for the students. An example was the visit to the Southwest Museum which is located very close to the Pasadena Freeway. It is a very good museum. Supposedly, it is the best west of the Mississippi! There is nothing more I can say about that!

The other experience that I was able to suggest and which the parents accepted was that the American buffalo which is among the American Indians a very important symbolic creature, so that when I told them that on the Island of Catalina, there are about 250 bison or buffalo, they said, "Let's go see the buffalo." And, we did! We took the Catalina Express from Long Beach to Avalon where a bus was waiting. We drove along the rim of the Catalina Island, and yes, there was a herd of buffalo. These animals are big! They are not always friendly. My wife and I had encounters with them privately when not with this group. However, the kids were thrilled to see Tatanka. It was a very successful outing. I still have contact with some of the parents of this Indian Education group, especially Lee Henderson, the Chairperson. I stayed with the ABC School District until 1988.

Iron Eyes Cody helps with Indian Education Program

17

Sailing

Everybody knew by now that I was a horseman. What one didn't know is that there was a family by the name of Shepardson. They were my customers in Long Beach where I was Riding Master at the Equestrotel Riding Stables. The Shepardson's were sailors, and they always kept asking me, "Wouldn't you and your wife like to go sailing with us?"

I really had a certain amount of apprehension about being seasick, so I always turned them down. One nice day, it happened that Hildburg, my wife, stood right next to me when the invitation was forthcoming. Before I could say "no" again, my wife had said yes. The Shepardson's did know what my commitments were as far as horse shows or when I was tied up on weekends, so they would always call about seven in the morning. Usually Hildburg would answer the phone. "Would you guys like to go sailing with us?" they would ask. I was totally out of the loop, and yes we did go sailing. We went sailing a lot.

Finally, I got to the point where I told Hildburg, "If we want to go sailing, let's go sailing when we want to, not when somebody invites us." So I did the first major mistake that sailors tend to do. I went to Ernie Wenk. He was a noted boat broker at Shelter Point in San Pedro. I said,

"Ernie, we've been going sailing with the Shepardson's but it might not be a bad idea if Hildburg and I had our own boat." He said, "I've got the boat for you!" It was a wooden hard chime Shutt, a 24-footer. It was a very fast boat.

Shutt 24 Raubauts

When the herd of boats headed back to the slips at the end of a sailing date, the Cal 25, the Coronado 25, and the Cal 20 were all charging back into the harbor. These guys just could not believe their eyes when they saw me bearing down on them and passing with my 24-foot wooden boat. We improved the boat. We put in a real head, and not just a porta potty. It was a nice boat.

But, I discovered one thing when we got back into port. When everybody else was up in the Clubhouse enjoying refreshments, I was still drying out the bilge and wood below deck. Well, that is the disadvantage of having a wooden boat. So, Hildburg and I decided to go and look for a fiberglass boat because we didn't want to spend our nights drying off the timbers below deck.

Catalina Caper

After Hildburg and I had purchased the Shutt 24, we came to the conclusion that when you have a boat, you have to go to Catalina. So, we invited Ed Shepardson. He was experienced enough to go with us to Catalina. Hildburg, Ed, and I sailed over to Avalon. We had one anchor and dropped our anchor, but we didn't have a second anchor!

However, we were free and clear from interfering with other boats. Ed and I decided it would be best to let Hildburg have the boat so that she could get ready for the night. Ed and I would go on shore and get ourselves ready for the evening. As we returned with the water taxi and we were trying to locate our boat, we noticed that there was a boat out there in the far harbor. Somebody on board of that boat was frantically using the flashlight to signal. As we approached closer and closer, I recognized the boat, and I said to the taxi man, "That's our boat over there." He said, "No, no, never mind. Forget about that. There's a lady on board and she thinks she is adrift and she is dragging her anchor. But, she is not, she is solid." I said, "No, no, that's my wife. That is my boat." So, he took us there and Hildburg was indeed quite relieved that we had returned. We settled down for the night, had a highball, and the next morning we were up and we returned back to San Pedro. That was the first time Hildburg and I spent the night on our boat in Catalina. Catalina is a special place.

One day I looked in the newspaper and saw an ad for a Cal 28. The price seemed ridiculously low, and I thought we could afford it. But, I wasn't going to have two boats. For this reason, Hildburg and I drove to Marina Del Rey. We went to the broker. By golly, there was that Cal 28 with an outboard, no lifelines, but good sails. The boat's name was

"Auspicious". It had been a very successful boat belonging to Rob Batcher in San Diego. The broker and I kind of agreed, and I said, "There's only one catch." He said, "What?" I said, "I have a boat and you'll have to take it on trade or we have no deal." He looked at me and said, "Well, we'll go ahead with that understanding." I said, "Wait a minute. Send one of your people down to look at my boat because I don't want to sail that boat up from San Pedro to Marina Del Rey and have you tell me 'no deal'".

So he did send a woman down and she was good sailor. She got right to the core of my boat's problem.

Cal 28 Auspicious

She reported back to her employer and told him that there was dry rot in the main timber. So, I asked the broker, "Do we have a deal, or do we not?" To my surprise, he said, "We have a deal." Before he could change his mind, I sailed my boat, "Raubauts". The name was based on a German horse named in a very classic story in Germany. I sailed Raubauts up to Del Rey, got out, handed the broker my check, got the pink slip, turned around and off we went to San Pedro where the slip I had for my Raubauts would be occupied by the Cal 28 named "Auspicious". And it was the start of an auspicious adventure!

Hildburg and I sailed the Auspicious back down to San Pedro. We were kind of wondering why in the world nobody was out sailing. We didn't realize that by the time we came into the harbor of San Pedro that we had Santa Ana conditions. We got knocked on to our side a number of times. I had a bit of a problem with the outboard motor. For that reason, we had to be very careful as we sailed into Fleitz Brothers Marina. The good news was that I had an upwind-slip and for that reason, it all went well. I now had what I would consider a quality boat. Modern technology throughout and she was very fast.

I added a bow pulpit and a stern pulpit, and lifelines to make her safe and comfortable. I was egged on and started racing the inverted race that the Cabrillo Beach Yacht Club (CBYC) puts on.

It was funny! Colleagues from Arcadia High School came to help me, but we were a half hour late getting to the starting line. I had to wait until everyone else had started. So, as a result, it was not what I would call an "Auspicious" beginning of a racing career with sailboats! But, we had fun.

While at Arcadia, the Arcadia Student Body Council had a habit of going to Newport to make their plans for student activities and the like for the ensuing school year. Being a show-off, Hildburg and I spent about a week to ten days in Catalina during the summer vacation period. We sailed into Newport Harbor where I had made some arrangements to moor my boat at a Yacht Club in Newport. Again, I was a little late getting there, but everybody was very thrilled and enthusiastic and the kids came over to the boat. We had a good time.

"Auspicious" became in a sense a savings, a piggy bank. We paid off the boat. The equity in the boat enabled us to pay off our home, and that gave me quite a bit more flexibility as far as planning for a career in education was concerned. I was now obviously hooked on boating.

It was after I had sold the Auspicious, Hildburg and I bought a Cal 20 we named "Seabiscuit". Cal 20s are excellent sailors but after you have been on a 28-footer, a 20-footer is a little bit cramped. We sold our Cal 20, and later on we went shopping for a somewhat larger boat. We ended up buying an Excalibur 26-footer. The name of the boat was "Hollywinds". We picked that boat up in San Diego. Hildburg and I sailed that boat up the coast into San Pedro.

Since 1972, Hildburg and I had belonged to the CBYC in San Pedro. We raced and enjoyed our stay there. As time went by, my sister discovered that I had a strong interest in real sailboat racing. The best thing about a sailboat is that you don't have to use it every day. You can leave it sit for a week or a month. Now and then, you have to start the engine and/or have the bottom "scraped." Other than that, it was a very practical and realistic solution for the situation that we were in.

Over the years, my sister and I, having grown up basically apart from one another, warmed up our relationship through our boating, and we became not just brother and sister but good friends.

One nice day, my sister said, "George, wouldn't you like to really go on a big boat." I said, "Sure, who wouldn't."

She said, "Well, I tell you what. You go and pick out a boat that you can take on the Transpacific Yacht Race (Transpac)." I said, "Wow, that's a big boat and it costs a lot of money." She said, "Don't worry, you're covered."

At that time when we were living in Glendale, and across the street from us lived George Griffith's mother-in-law. George Griffith was very much involved with the Jensen's, the Cal Boat Manufacturers. So, I sat down with him. He told me one thing that to this day I still have written behind my ears, "Don't ever make a mistake on a sailboat, it may be the last one you ever make." Whoopee! Then, he added, "So, you want to go on the Transpac?" I said, "What about a Cal 40?" You could get them at a more reasonable cost at that time. He said, "No, they are out designed." Now, I came across that problem you have with sailboat racing. They have formulas, and they have a design formula. At any rate, he said, "George, what you need to do is to go get yourself a CF 37." I asked, "What's that?" He said, "That's a very good boat and they have been dominating the races on the West Coast here in California and the Mexican waters. There have been some that have been very successful in doing the Transpac." So, I got in touch with Ed Feo, a banker by profession. He showed me his boatyard and his production site. Craig Belden, who is now a broker in Long Beach, was in charge of the manufacturing aspect. The quality of the boats was superior. At that point in time, racing sailboats were getting lighter and lighter and the lightest would go faster and faster and faster. The notion being, especially in these races like the Mexican races or the Transpac, that you tended to be surfing rather than having the hull deep in the water. The extremely fast boats, like the Hobie Cats and the Lee 50s, surfed!

What was reassuring to me was when Ed Feo said, "George, this boat will see you through heavy weather." That was good news for my wife and my sister didn't mind that either. So in the end, Hildburg and I had a Hull #29 and that became the first of a whole series of boats that we named "Sunburst."

The reason that all of my succeeding boats were "Sunburst", along with the accessories like the lifejackets, shirts, uniforms, etc., is that I kept the best. When I sold the boats, I sold the less desirable accessories. So, there I was with this new CF 37 called "Sunburst".

CF 37 Sunburst

We did a few races, but nothing too spectacular. This was probably due to the fact that the Skipper, yours truly, was not so skilled in going at the starting line, jibing, and tacking and doing all these things. I did develop a certain talent to attract crew members. There was Eric Bartow and there was a whole number of people who sailed with me in the many years that followed.

It must have been early 1981 and we were participating in the Pacific Handicap Racing Fleet (PHRF) Race sponsored by the Los Angeles Times. This was a series of races. This particular race was largely confined between the Point Fermin Buoy and the Long Beach Harbor Entrance Buoy. As we gathered at the Sunburst which I had moved to Long Beach for the race, the winds had built to gale force and were blowing 35mph or stronger. The Race Committee reminded the various skippers who were participating that it was their decision to continue to participate in view of these weather conditions.

It was a bleak morning. My regular crew and I were standing near the Sunburst, as was Hildburg. I finally made the Skipper's decision and told Hildburg that she could either go to the Club or she could go to a nearby restaurant but no matter what happened she was not going on this race because it was really hectic. The boats were heeling in the slips with the force of the wind on the bare poles! Hildburg was somewhat dejected. She waved us goodbye as we pulled out of the slip and headed toward the starting line. What I did not know was that the Cannonball was short of crew.

The Cannonball was a boat that was about 30' to 40' longer than our Sunburst. It was a black hulled, heavy solid ship. A lot of her regular crew just didn't show up. They felt the weather was too hazardous to go out. Her skipper, I don't remember his name, did what most of us do when we are short-handed. We go around the dock and see if we can find an able-bodied person who knows something about sailing. He approached Hildburg, and he said, "Lady, are you a sailor?" Hildburg said, "Yes." He then added, "Would you like to go out sailing?" Hildburg responded, "Yes." So, she got on the Cannonball!

Here we are at sea on a spinnaker run heading from Point Fermin to the Long Beach Entrance Buoy. If you are in a race, especially in heavy weather, you have to pay close attention to sail, water, and wind. I was in deep concentration.

Then, my crew said, "George, look!" I said, "What's up?" They said, "The Cannonball is coming!" I said, "I've seen the Cannonball before.

Besides, she is in a different class." The crew said, "No, George, look! You've never seen the Cannonball like this!" As the Cannonball was passing us, there was Hildburg in the cockpit, waving to us as she was going by! That little gal had more guts and courage than I had ever given her credit for. My sister knew that! She had said, "You know it took a lot of guts for that girl to leave her safe nest in Germany and follow that "penniless American soldier" to the United States." This meant that she had a lot of confidence in me.

The Sunburst sailed on and we did our thing. The Cannonball did her thing. And, Hildburg was waiting for us when we pulled into the slip!

I wanted to go on the Transpac, but I was told politely but firmly, "Young man! You don't have enough experience to go on the Transpac!" "What do I have to do to get the experience? I've won the City of Ensenada trophy going from Newport to Ensenada." They said, "That does not count! That is a local race. You have to have blue-water experience". I asked, "What would qualify for that?" They said, "Well, there is a race from Los Angeles, to Mazatlan, Mexico." I said, "Ay, yai, yai! Okay, sign me up!"

So, Sunburst went on her real blue-water maiden voyage and we sailed to Mazatlan. As it is on these long races, when you approach the finish line, you have to alert the Race Committee on their boat. When we called in, we had to tell them we were about an hour away from finishing in Mazatlan. On the way down to Mazatlan, we had a "round down" off Cabo San Lucas. If you don't know what a "round down" is, let me tell you what it is. You are surfing along on a big wave, and suddenly you're boat is back-winded and you go spinnaker pole first into the water. I have to say one thing, it pays to have a good crew because in three minutes the Sunburst was upright and racing again.

We had a new spinnaker up and the old one had been hauled in. The crew packed it and it would be ready if we needed it. Again, it was hard work! But, we did announce our arrival. We were on the radio listening to what traffic there was.

A present of the crew

George Griffith who had steered me to the CF 37 asked, "How is the Sunburst doing?" The word that he got from the Committee Boat was, "They are about a few minutes away from finishing." That meant that George Griffith, instead of being third, was fourth. Dennis Conner took first, Dennis Choate who built CF 37s, took second, and the Sunburst was third. We got a trophy. It was very exhilarating to come across the finish line and listen to some of the expletive deleted comments on the air.

I remember when we were pulling into Mazatlan, Dennis Conner was near the Mazatlan Yacht Club. As we passed his boat, he said, "Guys, you did a good job." We got a compliment from that Master. A lot of people said they didn't like him because he was supposedly stuck-up. Well, he knows how to sail, and he knows he knows! So, when you are in a race with Dennis Conner, you can pretty well figure that he has got the first place situated.

On our way down the Mexican coast, we came past a situation where from a distance, I wasn't so sure that it wasn't a fishing village at the horizon. It was night, and I spoke to my navigator, Rob Wallace. He swore it was not a shoreline. But, he did get on the radio, and it happened to be a Mexican naval cruiser that was out there. We asked them if we were on the proper course and they said we were doing fine. It was very, very satisfying to finish that race very successfully.

Later on when we were getting ready for the Transpac, during the summer months, I took one shower too many. I slipped and fell and broke my knee, but I was ready to answer the bell when we took off for the Transpac. After all, that was the purpose of the whole exercise.

On the Transpac adventures, I had a very good friend, Dave Robertson. His girlfriend at the time was Anita Braves, a colleague of mine in the ABC School District. Dave had indicated to Anita that he would like to sail with me on the Transpac. So, we did sail. I have to say one thing about Dave. A better navigator you couldn't get and a better cook you couldn't get and a better all-around hand you couldn't get. Later on, he became fame when sailing for Lowell North on the Four Deck, he walked on top of the spinnaker pole forward and changed spinnakers. That by itself is a feat. But, to do that in the San Francisco Bay Area in heavy winds is astounding!

As we approached the starting line to the Transpac, the crew members on my boat said, "George, there is a problem. We are dragging something." Yes, we had caught something on our rudder. It was a huge piece of kelp. Dave went into the water on the starboard side while we were moving towards the starting line. With two yanks, he had freed the boat of the kelp and he popped out of the water coming aboard on the port side. He was a little wet, but a towel dried him up quickly. I had a fantastic crew. I'll never forget them!

We had agreed that we were going to follow the Rhumb Line to Honolulu. There was one other CF 37 in this race, and that was Medicine Man which was skippered by Bob Lane. Bob is a very capable skipper. His crew was constantly complaining because he drove them very hard.

From my point of view, the only mistake Bob made was that he went south to pick up the trade winds instead of staying on the Rhumb Line which we did because we had all the wind we could handle. We were on the 2,500 mile trip to Hawaii.

Bill Murray was on the Transpac with me. He was a racing skipper in his own right, he knew what he was doing, he knew what he was talking about and her new celestial navigation. The first night out, we had lost one spinnaker. We couldn't understand why, but we had our second spinnaker up. Bill Murray said, "George, come up here. I'll be darned. Look! Look!" So, I scrambled up to where he was standing. He was handling the sheet for the spinnaker, and he pointed to the headstay. "Do you see what I'm seeing?" he asked. I said, "What do you see?"

He said, "You see those screws sticking out? You had the North Sails people put these screws in because it would hold the headfoils together when going toward weather, but on a spinnaker downwind run the headfoil is kind of just sliding back and forth." Another disappointment and I was the "guilty one."

That night Rick Sanders took the helm and Andy Glissell supervised. Jim Lucas went up the mast in the night, came down on the forestay in our boatswain's chair, and took all the screws out that I had paid bookoo money for to the North Sails people. When the screws were out, he got down, and now we were again under sail. We only had three more spinnakers left. One was a half-ounce chute tri-radial which was only good in extremely light air. We had a three-quarter ounce tri-radial which was at the borderline where we kind of figured that the winds were too strong for it as well. Then, we had the storm chute which was a reaching chute that was 1-1/2 ounce. We put that up, and it held. Hildburg, who wasn't there, later on said that it were the German colors on that chute, which I had bought secondhand from Roy Condiff, my advisor at North Sails that held the chute. We used that chute all the way to the finishing line in Honolulu.

One thing is certain. If you think you have everything planned to the tilt and hilt, something is going to go wrong. If something can go wrong, it will. So it was that on this run we had one bent spinnaker pole. The good news was that we had a second one, and we were able to use it.

Just arrived in Honolulu! Left to right: Hildburg,
author, Florence, Honolulu—Hostess

Hildburg did not go along on that trip. She was over there waiting at the Ilia and Wakelin Hotel. There was a wonderful get-together with the family when my brother-in-law, Geo Miller, a one-time U.S. Subcommander, my sister, and Hildburg and I and the wonderful crew that I had with me had what we called the "first night in a port". It was terrific. It was an experience that only happens once in a lifetime.

Hildburg in front of Sunburst in Honolulu

While we were in Honolulu, Dave and I were walking along the waterfront. We sat down, and Dave, kind of in a shy manner, asked me, "George, you know I really have a crush on Anita." I told him, "Well, you know something? You don't have to be a genius to tell that you two are very much an item." He said, "George, do you think I should ask her to marry me?" I told Dave the following, "Hildburg and I met by chance in our life. You and Anita, Dave, are similarly situated. If I were in your position, I would marry the lady because she is a fine woman. And, you cannot do better." He looked at me for a while and didn't say a word. Soon thereafter, there was Mr. and Mrs. Dave and Anita Robertson. Hildburg and I were at their wedding. I believe it was in October. Hildburg and I were very happy for those two young people. To this date, I consider them to be among our best friends.

Dave did Hildburg the honor, when her remains were given to the Sea. That is something in life one has to recognize. When God gives you the opportunity, go for it! Remain true to thyself and above all thou cannot then be false to any other person.

Rob Wallace brought the boat back from Hawaii. Those of you who do not know the layout on the Pacific side, you have to sail due North for about 800 miles until you see the "sign" that says "turn right for the U.S.". You are about at the latitude of San Francisco. You are on a reach as you drift southeast. At any rate, they did get back into San Pedro. As soon as the boat got in, I had my diver check her out. We had a problem with delamination. But Ed Feo was a gentleman and he gave us no trouble in fixing the delaminated portion which was about 6' by 2'. Hildburg and I enjoyed many years on the big Sunburst as we referred to her. We spent a lot of time in Catalina and we did a lot of local racing. I hate to brag, but when our boat showed up at the starting line, ours was one of the boats to beat in the class. We were quite successful. We have a lot of trophies with which to brag. They testify to our winning ways.

As time was going by, I consulted Dave Robertson who is a professional rigger, and responded to his point of order, if you will. He said, "George, your boat has campaigned quite a bit. You are going to have to replace the rigging." I said, "Well, how much is that going to set me back?" He said, "A little over $22,000." From that point forward, Hildburg and I had decided that we were through with what I would call big-time racing, and we would go back to a 28 or 27-footer or at least a smaller boat. We put the Sunburst up for sale, and it coincided with my retirement from public education. We moved to Escondido. Nobody even showed an interest in our Sunburst. So, I moved the Sunburst to Shelter Island in San Diego. No sooner had the boat been put into its new slip, the brokers started calling me from Long Beach and Del Rey. About a month later the boat was sold.

Hildburg and I had sort of mixed feelings about selling this beautiful boat. But as it turned out the buyer painted the hull and renamed the boat. He called her, "Sailsman". As Hildburg and I stood there in the boatyard looking at that boat, Hildburg said, "You know, I am kind of glad that he changed the name". And, I agreed. Well, you don't live long without a boat once you've been accustomed to having a boat. We bought a Capri 25 from Monte Yearly in Oceanside.

Capri 25 Sunburst

What we had forgotten is that you have to stoop down when you go below deck. We were at that age now where you don't like stooping down. We eventually sold the Capri 25 and we purchased an Excalibur. The headroom was still marginal. Then, Hildburg's medical problem caught up with her.

18
Golfing versus Boating

As Hildburg and I were approaching circa 1988 and my retirement from public education, we were wondering what one does when one is retired? So, I looked at my sister and my brother-in-law, George Miller. They had elected to play golf. I figured if my sister could do it, I surely can! So I retired circa 1988. We sold our home in Glendale, and bought a home on the 5th Fairway of the Escondido Country Club where we thought we would be enjoying a happy life as time went by. And, we did have a happy life in Escondido.

We joined the Escondido Country Club, we became regular members, we bought a golf cart, and we bought a Big Bertha and all the goods and hardware that go with being a golfer. Hildburg and I started making moderate progress in our ability to play golf. What we did learn is that you have to take lessons, which we did. You have to focus, you have to concentrate, and you have to apply yourself. It is almost like a full-time job! During the time when I was purchasing the Big Bertha and all the equipment, I asked Howard, the Assistant Pro at the Escondido Country Club, if all of this was going to help me become a better golfer.

He said, "Mr. Richardson, at your level of accomplishment, it will take a lot more than just that!"

Hildburg my golfing partner

It was during these first two years that my cousin, Hartmut, from Hamburg and his wife, Hilke, came for a visit. They liked golf. They took it up. Believe it or not, they are good golfers now because of our influence. But, they applied themselves. And, that is where the difference was. Hildburg and I worked at playing golf. However, our interest in golf, divided with our interest in boating, became a real problem.

We found, as we were trying to schedule our tee-off, that we barely beat the associate members onto the first tee around noon. This did not make us too popular with many of them because they had to wait for us to get going. Some of those guys were long hitters! Believe me you do learn to respect their wrath.

At any rate, Hildburg and I decided to join the mob, so we abandoned our regular status and we became associates. This wasn't any better, we didn't play any better, and we were still dividing our time between our boats (we had two) and the golf course. The Escondido Country Club has a fantastic swimming pool and a Jacuzzi. All this gave us a fantastic opportunity to play retirees. So, it became quite obvious that it was becoming a tug-of-war between golf and boat. In golf we had achieved absolutely very little, and in boats we had a certain reputation, if you will. There was still a little Schnauzer, all 56 pounds of her loving affection, and she did need our attention.

For that reason between boat, golf, and Schnauzer, golf took the short-end of it. There just wasn't enough time to give the game of golf, on our part, the proper focus and attention. Therefore, the boat won out!

Hildburg and Bella in front of our
CAL 28 in Oceanside

We remain social members at the Escondido Country Club, and we continue our membership at the Cabrillo Beach Yacht Club (CBYC) where I still have good friends among the Old Guard. Come to think of it, I am entering into that now, too, where I am part of the Old Guard. That is life—you just have to get old.

19

Hildburg's Passing

It was in December 2005. We were at the Escondido Dog Park, when Hildburg said, "I'm having a bit of a problem with my breathing." She was a chronic asthmatic. She asked me if it was alright if she could go back to the car. About a half hour later I went back to the car with Noelle. She was not feeling well. Hildburg had an oxygen machine at home. She had a portable oxygen bottle that she would carry on trips. She had nothing that bothered her, really. We had an albuterol machine. She and I would go three times a week to the YMCA, which we had joined to work out and stay physically fit. However, fate caught up with us. One night or perhaps in the early morning, I don't remember, she said, "George, my medication is not doing me any good anymore. I think I have to go the hospital." I said, "Well, we're not going to debate that." So, I called 911, and Hildburg went to the hospital. Dr. Buetell and the Escondido Pulmonary Group looked after her at Palomar Hospital. It was a very difficult time for both her and me. Hildburg had flutes implanted in her lungs. She could not breathe by herself.

Prior to all of this and because of the tenuous health situation that she experienced, we established an Advanced Health Directive. Finally in early January 2006, I saw one of her doctors and I asked him if he had in his experience seen a person recover from Hildburg's condition? He waited a long time, shook his head, and then said, "No." Then, I asked him, "Had you read her advanced healthcare directive?" Reluctantly, he said, "Yes." Then I asked, "Are we at that point in time where we should implement this?" He said, "Well, yes." He was immediately going to order that the flutes and all of this stuff be taken out and to put her on morphine. I said, "Hold it. Hildburg is Roman Catholic. She is very devout, and I do want her to have the last rites of her Church." The doctor said, "We will wait until that is done." The priest came from the Church of St. Timothy, not her regular church but the other Catholic Church in Escondido. The priest was from the Philippines originally.

I did not hold that against him. He knew his stuff. Hildburg received the last rites. That was a tough thing. She was put on morphine, and the flutes were removed. Hildburg checked out at 6:58 p.m. on January 12th, 2006.

Prior to the cremation I arranged with the burial institute to have Noelle say farewell to Hildburg. We entered the hall and Noelle walked up to the corps, turned around and walked away. Suddenly she stopped, looked back over her shoulder and returned to Hildburg. She got on the chair next to her and shook her arm, that was hanging loose on Hildburg's side.

Recognizing, that Hildburg had died, Noelle turned and walked slowly away.

Hildburgs Memorial

We had a religious service in the Church of the Resurrection, and the Celebration of Life at the Escondido Country Club. Our friends from the CBYC in San Pedro came. The relatives from Texas and Pasadena came. Everybody knew she was a wonderful, wonderful person. I was going to miss her.

Elisabeth at the CBYC Yacht Harbor The CBYC-Committee-Boat getting ready to leave the landing.

Afterwards, the Cabrillo Beach Yacht Club set aside the Cabrillo, which was the Club's Committee boat. We all went out—my sister and my niece, Elisabeth, who flew in from Germany. It was a flotilla of boats with friends and well-wishers. We went out about 500 yards off the Point Fermin buoy. Dave Robertson attended to this chore. We committed Hildburg's remains to the Sea. Amen.

Dave Robertson and Florence Basket with Hildburg's
ashes being given to the sea

Dave and Elisabeth, leaving the burial site

20
Return to Europe in 2009

During the summer of 2009, I had finalized the legal and physical issues that were connected with Hildburg's checking out. I started making plans to make one more last trip to Dresden, Germany with stops in Hamburg and Oldenburg so that no one would feel left out. In order to do this, I had to lean on my good friend, Joe Yaglinski. It was only when Joe agreed that he was going to stay in the house and take care of Noelle, our cute little 56-pound Standard Schnauzer that I have, that I went forward and finalized my trip to Germany.

Cabrillio Beach Yachtclub, San Pedro.
Left to right: Dave und Anita Robertsons, Joe Yaglinski

Hamburg and Oldenburg

First, I flew into Frankfurt and then on to Hamburg, where I spent a delightful visit with my cousin, Hartmut and his wife, and the wonderful family that they have, their children and their grandchildren. We all had a delightful time. All good things come to an end.

So, I traveled to Oldenburg where I had quarters at Hotel Wieting. I figured that would afford me a degree of freedom, and I would not be so much of a burden on the daily on-goings at my niece, Elisabeth's home. She is a gracious hostess, but she has three horses, four dogs, three children, a husband and then me, Uncle George?

I thought that would be too much, so for that reason I stayed at the hotel. We got together when everybody's time permitted and we had a delightful time. I also had the opportunity to meet some of Elisabeth's friends.

Elisabeth showed me the area around Oldenburg and we drove to the Zwischenahner Meer. We wanted to have coffee in the restaurant of the "Zwischenahner Segelklub" and enjoy the view of the Zwischenahner Meer from the terrace.

Here we ran into Horst Gerdes, to whom I talked to for a long time. Then he invited me to go sailing with him on his boat.

A few days later I met his wife Magdalena.

Cardinal Clemens August Graf Von Galen

During my visit in 2009, I had the opportunity to travel in the back country of the District of Oldenburg and I was very impressed by the long history that radiates throughout that region. On that occasion, Elisabeth took me to Bethen where we looked at the church that was once the church of Hildburg's uncle through her mother. This was the Church of Cardinal Count Augustus Clemens Graf von Galen.

It was an austere, a rather Baroque, establishment reflecting the Cardinal's personal use. One has to keep in mind that he was running against the highest authorities in Germany at the time when he took the stand on the issue of "worthless human beings". That was the notion he would not accept, no matter what Hitler or other VIPs of that time were preaching. He stood his ground, and for that I respect him. The kind of character that the man demonstrated was also the kind of character that I admired in Hildburg, that wonderful lady.

August Clemens was elevated to be a Cardinal by Pope Pius. This was an episode and an excursion into the countryside that I will never forget. That man was a man of his conviction. He was quite a guy.

To give one an insight and perspective into the eminent role portrayed by Hildburg's maternal uncle, Cardinal Clemens August Graf von Galen, during Hitler's ten-year period as the Führer, there is a paragraph from Heinz Linge's memoirs below, "With Hitler to the End." Heinz Linge served as Hitler's valet following the outbreak of war in 1939 until Hitler's suicide on April 30th, 1945.

"Behind the scenes, in Hitler's closest circle, it was clear that there was water in the wine. Dr. Karl Brandt, Hitler's travelling physician, had returned the day before from Münster, where he had had a general discussion on the Jewish question with Cardinal Clemens August Graf von Galen. They also talked about public opinion on the war and the general mood amongst the German people. Brandt, hanged by the Americans at Landsberg Prison after being found guilty of crimes against humanity at Nuremberg, came back from Münster depressed. At the beginning of the war he had been given the job of organizing the euthanasia programme, the destruction of 'worthless lives', and the cardinal had impressed him deeply, something he made no attempt to conceal. 'My God', he said, 'if I told the Führer everything the cardinal said to me, the cardinal and I would both be in a concentration camp by morning.'"

Return to Dresden

From there on I flew to Klotzsche. It was totally a different feeling when I landed in Klotzsche. When I was a boy, I remember seeing the airplanes touching down and taking off from the airport. This time around, I pulled in first class, the taxi was there, and I was on my way to the hotel where I had a reservation. As a boy I remember that hotel because it was preempted by German officers and their families. It is still a first class hotel! It has to be, because I wouldn't have stayed there if it weren't.

It is also listed in the directory of Automobile Club of Southern California. I arrived in Klotzsche, checked in, and had a bite to eat. When I came down, the hotel clerk said I had a guest waiting. I said, "A guest? Harrumph." It turned out to be Eickert Lehman. I think the last time Eickert and I had seen each other was in 1944. I was Gefolgschaftsführer of the Riders H.J., District 100. He was Stammführer of the Hitler Youth Klotzsche and surrounding areas. Obviously, our paths took a different turn.

When the Russians, and I use this term cautiously, liberated the areas, that 16-year old Eickert was considered such a danger to the Soviet Military Machine, that he was interned for the succeeding five years in a Concentration Camp at Buchenwald. Eickert and I reminisced. I asked about many of my friends, the Pfeiffers and the others. He said, "No, none of them were seen after the War. In the Pfeiffers' case, they were able to get out of Germany, and joined up with their father in Argentina. But many others were just happy to get out of the Soviet zone." When we used the word "liberation", it brings to mind that Polish troops were so eager not to be liberated by the Russians that they carried the German equipment beyond the lines that had been set up at Yalta. Liberation was such that the war atrocities which were often attributed to the Nazis were in fact being also committed by the Red Army against the civilian population in Eastern Europe, Lithuania, Poland, and Czechoslovakia. Everybody was scared! If you made clear that you didn't believe the Russkies, you were on your way to Siberia. Well, they also had other places where they could use your labor until you collapsed out of exhaustion.

Across the street from where I used to live in Klotzsche, there was the Bannack Family. The street at that time was called Mutchmann Strasse, because Mutchmann was a Nationalist Socialist Gauleiter. It is now properly named the Geschwister-Scholl Strasse. Bannack was about six or seven years younger than I, and he lived across the street. I didn't quite learn nor was I going to pump and press how "liberation" went for him. At any rate, he still lived in the same house that his parents had. I am happy for him. The house was in excellent condition. We had a grand get together.

We then saw to it that others who had known me would be informed of my presence. Believe it or not, there was a gentleman in Klotzsche by the name of Gottfried Oertel. He was the son of the Lutheran pastor who had confirmed me. On that occasion, I gave him the letter which his father had sent my mother wherein it was obvious that he did not know that the donor was my mother who had sent relief packages to them during the postwar years.

While I was in Klotzsche, I traveled to Dresden. In Dresden, I have a cousin, Sieglinde. We traveled through the grand city of Dresden. I wanted to see the Semper Opera. Of course, they had ongoing renovations and therefore I could not see the Semper Opera. I saw, on the other hand, the Zwinger which is a world-class art museum. I also saw the school my mother attended. The schools which I attended had been wiped out during the war. We traveled through Dresden. One nice day, we went on a trip up to Elbe River. I almost forgot to mention that my cousin, Klaus, from Seeshaupt, Bavaria had come and took up quarters at the hotel where I was staying in Klotzsche.

Author with cousin Klaus

It turned out that all of us, Klaus, Sieglinde, and I took an Elbe River trip into what was called Rathen in the Sächsische Schweiz. I remember that cluster of mountains because there is a place (Rathen) where Karl May had these wonderful wild-west shows based on his imagination on how the Wild West was. It was a wonderful recreation. We then all returned, and I would not leave Dresden without having seen the Karl May Museum in Radebeul. The curator of the museum was an individual who had been constantly on the go, and who was in a sense more wild western than Old Shatterhand. He had traveled in the American West and he had seen the Dakota Tribes. He had an authentic buffalo robe depicting the battle of the Little Big Horn, supposedly the only one in existence. It is a fantastic museum with all kinds of Indian lore exhibits that brought me back to the days when I was young and yes, in fact, good looking!

It is a shame that Hildburg could not be with me on these trips because Hildburg and I, to quote my sister who said, "The two of you had grown up together." Hildburg is always with me in spirit wherever I go.

Upon returning from an excursion from the Weisser Hirsch going down along the line where normally one would have ridden Street Car No.11, I stopped at the Schloss Albrechtsberg. Here in the years of 1943 and 1944, the Hitler Youth Reiter H.J. would gather on Wednesdays and Saturdays. We had our formations, all 150 of us with over 28 horses in the barn together with a whole slew of maybe hundreds of rats (four legged). When I went up to where the riding ring had been, yes, there was still the open space but nothing had been done to maintain it. Where once the carriages and coaches were stored, the garages were now empty. But, where the horses once stood and the rats had a wonderful time, there was now a restaurant/beer joint. I don't know how they are getting along with the rats, because I am sure they must still be somewhere around inside the masonry of that establishment. It looked totally different. There was a totally different atmosphere there. There wasn't even a safe crossing where horses and pedestrians could have crossed the road. Time had wrought a drastic change. That era is gone forever and will never return.

As my stay in Dresden, Klotzsche came to an end, I invited all of my friends and relatives who I could locate to a get-together. Lehman couldn't make it, his wife was not well. Bannack and his wife came.

Mr. Oertel and his fiancé came. To this day I don't know if they have gotten married. My cousin, Klaus, was there. My other cousin, Sieglinde, came and her daughter, Simone, a very good-looking young lady who is married with children.

Boy, are they a good-looking family! We all got together at the hotel where we had a delightful aloha-type of dinner. Why do I say aloha, because that means hello and good-bye at the same time.

Aloha–Dinner
Left to right: Bannack, Sieglinde, Klaus und Simon

A quick trip to Paris

I had to cut my stay short in Dresden short by three or four days because my niece in Paris was a little hurt that I had not planned to visit her. So, I left Klotzsche via Vienna to Paris and I had some delightful days in Paris.

Susanna lives in Paris very close to the Eiffel Tower. She picked me up at the airport and we drove to her home. Her home has four flights with a roof garden, a typical Parisian domicile. Her husband, Tony van Hagen who is an international lawyer was there, and I met several of her children. I don't mean children because her son, Evan, was a young man who was going to college in England. The van Hagens have a home in Christchurch, England. They have a home in Paris and they have homes on the Riviera. They have a powerboat. The young man, i.e. Susanna's son, played polo. Susanna is a principal art promoter in Paris. She puts on big exhibits. She has a lot of influence. She knows the former French Premier, Jacques Chirac.

Overwhelmed in Paris, Susanne left, Toni and George on the right

We had a delightful time. The weather was perfect. One could sit outside in a café and have one's meals. There was always a group of people that Susanna had brought in. It was a wonderful way to remember the City of Lights.

That, too, came to an end. I did not get to meet her daughter who is following an art career and who was studying in Berlin at the time. Knowing her mother and father and having met her brother, I confidently predict that this young lady is going to have a fantastic career. It doesn't hurt that her mother is one of the leading persons in Paris.

My niece, Susanna, had an art show going on in Paris during the time I was visiting. So, when her presence was required there, she farmed me out to the Louvre. Hildburg and I had been to the Louvre many times. But, you know something? Every time you go back to that establishment, you will see things that you have never seen before or heard of before that will impress you!

Alas, my visit had to come to an end. Joe Yaglinski had made it quite clear that he was going to go to Catalina on a certain date because of a commitment that he had there. So, I had to get back to Escondido. I arrived in the middle of the night. Joe was sleeping and Noelle greeted me with all sorts of expressions of joy, squeals, barks, yelps. It was good to be home!

21

Summary

As I think back, my life had gone full circle, from the Midwest to Germany and back to the Midwest to California. In summing up my experiences, both in Germany and in the United States, I can say that as a youngster I was anti-Bolshevik in Germany, in my service in the Counterintelligence Corp and I was anti-Bolshevik in the United States. Throughout it all, there was one constant that I can claim to be mine and that was my involvement with youth, be it in the Hitler Youth, be it in the Jung Volk, be it in the schools that I was attending, be it with horses, and later with dogs and on sailboats.

2010 with Schnauzer Noelle

I have only met wonderful people. If people should turn out to be not so wonderful, I would quickly disengage myself from their presence. In my teaching, I followed the Confucius dictum, "I will teach one-third and hope that those I am teaching will make clear unto themselves the remaining two-thirds or I will not teach them again." In public education, there was no way one could carry that out. In the Equestrian field, I can say that I had two outstanding students, Carol Hancock and Kay Switzer, who won the California State Equestrian Championships in different years at the Cow Palace in San Francisco. Carol was a walk/trot, i.e., a gaited rider and Kay Switzer was a Hunter Jumper. It was a fantastic experience working with young people. I have also told the young people not to worry about people not knowing them but that they should worry about whether or not they are worth knowing.

Another dictum that I repeated again, based on the Chinese scholar, is "If you have made a mistake and do not set about to correct it, you have already made another mistake." It is amazing how much kids remember those little quips.

Two decades after I had left L.A. High, I was in Cerritos at a service station, when a Black gentleman came to me and he asked, "Excuse me, sir, are you not Mr. Richardson who taught at L.A. High?" I said, "Yes, I am." He said, "Sir, I will never forget you." To me as a teacher, that was the best compliment one could ever have!

At this point in my life, I am now sailing an Ericson 27. The nice thing about that boat is that I can stand up straight in the main cabin. I can go from the main cabin into the enclosed head without having to stoop down.

Partytime on my Ericson 27 „Sunburst" in Oceanside

I have a self-furling headsail, and I have all sorts of reefing gizmos, gimmicks on the mainsail and a Yanmar Diesel. So that at my age, and I am over 84, I can enjoy the days that remain with my faithful little Schnauzer, Champion K.B's Sing Noel von Stocker (aka Noelle).

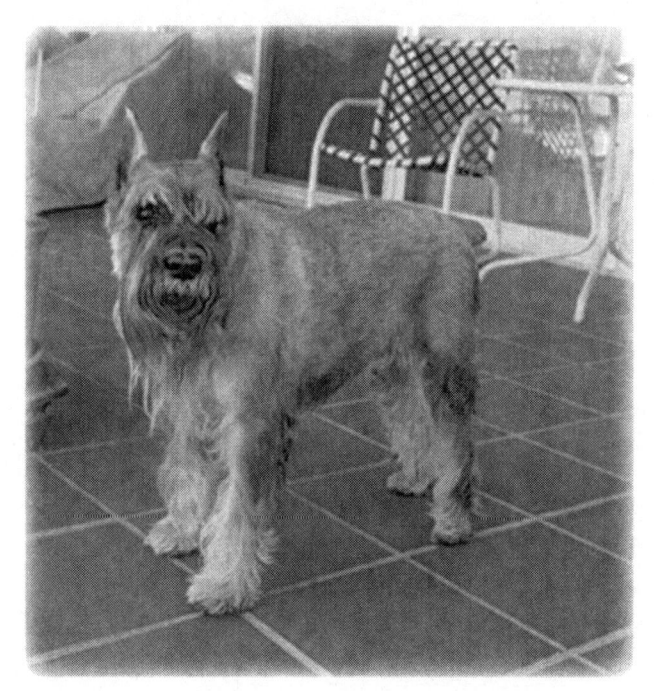

Schnauzer Champion K.B. Noelle von Stocker

I am in awe of God. I do not think that God is particularly loving and kind to people. There are billions of people whose prayers, if I am right, he cannot listen to! Hildburg and I are of the conviction that in that time beyond we are going to meet again and be together. If there is no hereafter, then that which she and I experienced together, every moment of that life I had with this wonderful lady, was yes, "Under Two Flags", the German Flag and the American Flag, from the horse to the canine, to the seagulls. I have no regrets. I thank my sister, Florence, for the support she has showed me in the closing months of Hildburg's life. I was singularly blessed.

Epilogue

Magdalena Bergen-Gerdes   Bad Zwischenahn

In February/March 2013

Dear George,

On the day, when Horst moored up with his Tempest at the Zwischenahner Segelklub and enjoyed his drink on the terrace, our steady life style changed.

In the summer of 2009 you and your niece Elisabeth stopped off the club and engaged in a conversation with Horst.

During the discussion Horst praised the island of Helgoland, while you spoke of Catalina, an island about 20 miles southwest of San Pedro.

After a short sail with you on the Zwischenahner Meer a lasting friendship was sealed.

Our love for America developed rapidly, and in a short time you americanized us.

In the following summer holidays our enthusiasm for America was renewed and deepened. This meant that the decades long passion for yachting was pushed into the background. We were able to read your book on the occasion of our second summer vacation in 2011 with you.

It again brought us back pleasant memories of you on your terrace with the beautiful view of the golf course and we heard your exciting and informative stories from your past life. With your help we were able to gain incomparable and unforgettable impressions of California, Arizona and Nevada, which we have taken home with us.

On this occasion we would like to thank you and Noelle (your sweet Standard Schnauzer) for your faithful friendship and wonderful hospitality.

Horst und Magdalena

Bibliography

Linge, Heinz, *With Hitler to the End, the Memoirs of Adolf Hitler's Valet,* Frontline Books, London/Skyhorse Publishing, New York 1980.

CPSIA information can be obtained at www.ICGtesting.com
Printed in the USA
LVOW06s0259200713

343770LV00001B/71/P